An Issue of the Heart

THE NEUROPSYCHOTHERAPIST
SPECIAL ISSUE

Edited by Matthew Dahlitz & Geoff Hall

Chapters in this edition have previously been published in *The Neuropsychotherapist*.

For information about content reproduction write to: Permissions, The Neuropsychotherapist, PO Box 1030, Park Ridge, QLD, 4125, Australia.
Alternatively email editor@neuropsychotherapist.com

Editor-in-Chief: Matthew Dahlitz
Associate Editor: Geoff Hall

Cover image: ktsdesign/Bigstockphoto.com

Title: An Issue of the Heart: The Neuropsychotherapist Special Issue.

ISBN-13: 978-1508838746 (paperback)
ISBN-10: 1508838747

1. Psychotherapy. 2. Heart. 3. Neuroscience. 4. Heart-Brain. 5. Heartmath.

Printed in the United States of America

NEUROPSYCHOTHERAPIST.COM

Preface

A WONDER OF COMPLEXITY IS THE HUMAN BEING—something that continues to be a source of fascination and frustration for those of us who have set ourselves to understand human behaviour. This special issue focuses on the heart, an organ with a profound influence over our mental lives. We are all familiar with the heart in its classical biological role as pump circulating vital oxygenated blood through the body. But how many are versed in its neural and bioelectromagnetic influence upon our brains? Research has revealed the heart even radiates an influence on those around us via electromgnetic fields. In the past such claims might have been dismissed as mere New Age fancy, but with ever more sophisticated and sensitive instruments, formal studies in recent years have demonstrated that our bodies have amazing multidimensional fields of awareness and influence.

These findings about the heart continue to add weight to the argument that in the counselling room it is the therapist's unconditional positive regard, warmth, and personal coherence more than any technique that make for effective therapy. It makes one wonder what the focus of training should be for new therapists—will courses become more focused on students developing personal coherence, practising attitudes of genuine care and compassion, and understanding what they are radiating to clients from their hearts?

Neuropsychotherapy, and the multidisciplinary integration that it stands for, is part of an important paradigm shift in medicine. Likewise, the focus on matters heart–brain in this issue reflects an important shift of understanding in the broader field of health. The study of any one bodily system—even the central nervous system in the case of psychologists—leaves us in the dark on many levels for many phenomena. It is my hope that you will come to appreciate the wonderful, so often implicit influence the heart has on our emotions and relationships, and that we will become more conscious of being authentic and coherent—for our clients and also for ourselves.

When you tell a client that you "hear" his or her "heart", you are probably being more literal than you realise. And bear in mind that your client can likely "hear" your heart just as loudly.

Matthew Dahlitz
Brisbane
March 2015

iii

Contents

WHY THE HEART IS MUCH MORE THAN A PUMP

Paul J. Rosch, MD, FACP

According to standard dictionaries, the heart is:

A hollow muscular organ that pumps the blood through the circulatory system by rhythmic contraction and dilation.

The organ in your chest that pumps blood through your veins and arteries.

The chambered muscular organ in vertebrates that pumps blood received from the veins into the arteries, thereby maintaining the flow of blood through the entire circulatory system.

None of these definitions are correct, since it is impossible for the heart to pump blood through the entire circulatory system. Ventricular contraction forces blood into the aorta and pulmonary artery, but these vessels become progressively smaller and end in 25,000 miles of capillaries. Some of these have a diameter not much larger than a red blood cell, and if laid end to end, the capillary system would cover the area of three football fields. The heart could never pump air through this complicated network, much less a viscous fluid like blood, since this would require a force or pressure capable of lifting a 100-pound weight 1 mile high.

The Medieval "Medical Pope"
Who Dominated Western and Muslim Medicine

The ancient Greeks, and especially Claudius Galen, attributed all diseases to some imbalance in the four humors: blood, phlegm, black bile, and yellow bile. All of these circulated throughout the body due to the innate heat (*calidum innatum*) generated by the heart. The heart's heat was also responsible for extracting each humor from various foods in order to maintain a healthy equilibrium. Galen believed that "vital blood" was made by the heart and flowed through the arteries to carry the vital spirits. This was different from "nutritive blood", which was made by the liver and carried through veins to body organs that consumed it to provide energy. He also believed that blood passed through the septum of the heart from one ventricle to the other through tiny invisible pores, rather than arteries. Blood flowed from the liver to the right ventricle of the heart and nourished the lungs via the veins. The left ventricle nourished the rest of the body through arteries that he thought were air pipes, but also contained vital spirits. In addition, the heart did not pump blood, but sucked it in from the veins. The rise and fall of the pulse came from a contraction and relaxation that originated in the arteries rather than from any pumping action of the heart.

It is impossible to overestimate the power Galen has had over medicine. He was such an unquestioned authority that he was later referred to as "The Medical Pope of the Middle Ages". Few of his writings had at the time been preserved for physicians, although they were translated into Arabic in the 11th century, particularly by Ibn Sina, or Avicenna as he was later known in the West. Avicenna was a child prodigy who memorized the Koran and Arabic poetry by the age of 10, was fluent in several languages, and wrote some 400 books or tracts. The most famous was his *Qanun*, or The Canon of Medicine, completed in 1025. Its 14 volumes containing over one million words covered every conceivable aspect of medical practice gleaned from ancient Persian, Indian and Arabic texts, but it was primarily a tribute to all of Galen's teachings and views. Its 1593 publication in Rome made it one of the first Arabic books to be printed and further enhanced Galen's authority, because it was now widely available. From the 12th to 18th century, the *Qanun* was the most important medical text in the world because of its encyclopedic comprehensiveness and systematic arrangement. It is believed to have influenced Leonardo Da Vinci. Sir William Osler wrote, "The *Qanun* has remained a medical bible for a longer time than any other work", and the Encyclopedia Britannica described it as "the single most important book in the history of medicine, East or West".

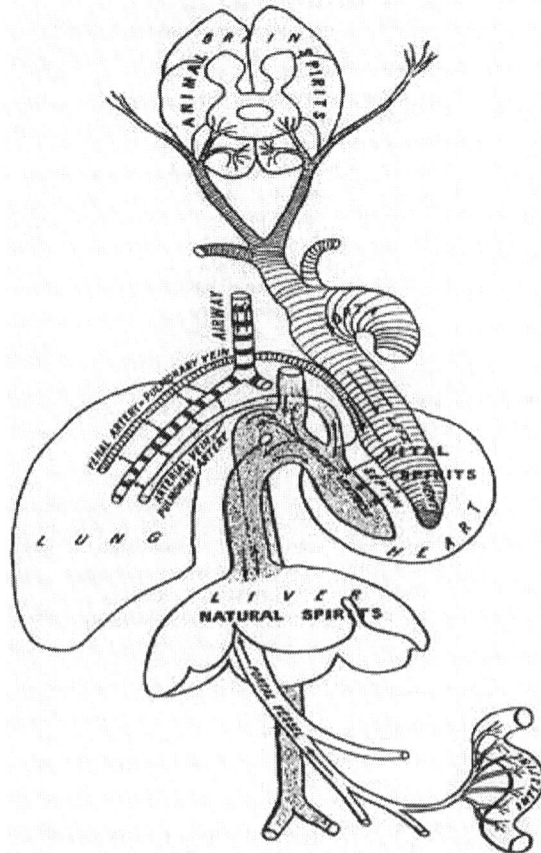

A Galen illustration of the internal organs depicting his concepts of anatomy and spirit.

The natural healing principles described in the *Qanun* were studied by Samuel Hahnemann, founder of homeopathy, as well as Father Sebastian Kneipp, who established naturopathy. Some of Galen's recommendations to restore the balance of the four humors, such as bleeding, cupping, leeches, purging and sweating were standard practices well into the 19th century. George Washington's quinsy (bad sore throat) was treated by bleeding, and he had an additional two quarts of blood removed on the day he died in December, 1799. The 1899 edition of the Merck Manual, the most popular textbook of the day for physicians and pharmacists (for $1.00), included bleeding as an accepted treatment, and this and others such as cupping are still widely used in parts of the world. Even some alleged folk remedies of rural Afro-Americans have been traced back to medicinal recipes from Avicenna's *Qanun*, or Canon as it is often referred to. Phlebotomy, or bleeding, is currently used to treat hemochromatosis to remove excess iron, and surgeons often utilize leeches when reattaching severed body parts such as fingers, after tissue grafts, and to reduce hematomas following plastic surgery.

William Harvey's *De Motu Cordis*, Ibn al-Nafis, Michael Servetus, and the Church

The belief that the heart pumped the blood through the arteries and veins is usually attributed to William Harvey, but this is also erroneous. In his famous 1628 *Exercitatio Anatomica de Motu Cordis et Sanguinis in Animalibus* (On the Motion of the Heart and Blood in Animals), Harvey demonstrated (a) that it was the contraction, not the dilatation of the heart that coincided with the pulse; (b) that the pulse was not produced by the arteries enlarging and contracting but by being filled with blood with each contraction; (c) there was no pulsation in the veins, but rather a constant stream of blood from the periphery to the heart; (d) the blood in the arteries was the same as that in the veins; (e) there were no pores in the septum between the ventricles; (f) the action of the right and left auricles and ventricles and the valves between them is the same with respect to the reception and propulsion of liquid, not air, since the blood on the right side, although mixed with air, is still a liquid; and (g) blood in the right ventricle is sent to the lungs, returns to the left atrium via the pulmonary veins and is then sent into the arteries and returns through veins that empty into the vena cavae, which return it to the right side of the heart to complete its circulation. Simply put, blood flowed in one direction throughout the body and it was in the lungs where the transformation of venous blood to arterial blood took place. Whereas Galen believed that the liver was the center of circulation, Harvey found no evidence that blood was manufactured in or secreted by the liver, and calculated that if Galen had been correct, the liver would have to produce 540 pounds of blood daily.

Although Harvey announced his discovery in 1615, he waited 13 years before publishing his results, since it was considered sacrilegious to challenge Galen. Any contrary opinions were considered to be so heretical that they would not only quickly end one's career, but could result in being burned at the stake. The celebrated physician and anatomist Andreas Vesalius had published his *De Humani Corporis Fabrica* in 1543, which disputed Galen's description of the heart and liver, and was condemned by the church for dissecting a human corpse. In 1553, a Spanish doctor and theologian, Michael Servetus, published *Christianismi Restitutio* (The Restoration of Christianity), which also opposed many of Galen's ideas. This was during the Spanish Inquisition. He was burned at the stake, together with a copy of his book, for his heresy. It seems likely that Servetus was strongly influenced by Ibn al-Nafis, Chief Physician at the Al-Mansouri Hospital in Cairo and physician to Egypt's Sultan. As with many other Muslim physicians of his time, not only did Al-Nafis excel in medicine, but he was also well versed in several languages, philosophy, Islamic law, and history, and wrote numerous works disputing both Galen and Avicenna.

One of Al-Nafis' most important books, the 20-volume *Commentary on Anatomy in Avicenna's Canon*, written in 1242, explained that there were only two ventricles, not three; there were no pores through the interventricular septum, and the ventricle received its nourishment from the coronary vessels, not, as Galen and Avicenna had claimed, from blood deposited in the right ventricle. His premonition of a precursor to capillary circulation was due to his discovery that "the pulmonary vein receives what comes out of the pulmonary artery, this being the reason for the existence of perceptible passages between the two." Al-Nafis was an early proponent of experimental medicine, postmortem autopsy, and human dissection, at which he excelled. He drew several diagrams of his new physiologic system, some of which have been preserved, but his skill and ingenuity are evident in the following excerpt.

The blood from the right chamber of the heart must arrive at the left chamber, but there is no direct pathway between them. The thick septum of the heart is not perforated and does not have invisible pores as Galen claimed. The blood from the right chamber must flow through the pulmonary artery to the lungs, spread through its substances, be mingled there with air, pass through the pulmonary vein to reach the left chamber of the heart, and there form the vital spirit. The heart has only two ventricles . . . and between these two there is absolutely no opening. Also dissection gives this lie to what they said, as the septum between these two cavities is much thicker than elsewhere. The benefit of this blood (that is in the right cavity) is to go up to the lungs, mix with what is in the lungs of air, then pass to the left of the two cavities of the heart.

Al-Nafis also disproved Galen's theory that "every part of an artery pulsates "simultaneously" and that the motion of the pulse was due to "the arteries expanding and contracting naturally". He attributed the pulse to the force of cardiac contraction, noting that "the arteries and the heart do not expand and contract at the same time, but rather the one contracts while the other expands" and vice versa. He also recognized that the purpose of the pulse was to help disperse the blood from the heart to the rest of the body. All of these observations were made almost 400 years before Harvey, who was unable to explain how blood was transferred from arteries to veins. None of these important observations were known in Europe until 1547, when Andrea Alpago translated some of Al-Nafis' writings into Latin. Six years later, Michael Servetus described the pulmonary circulation in his book: "air mixed with blood is sent from the lungs to the heart through the arterial vein; therefore, the mixture is made in the lungs. The bright color is given to the sanguine spirit by the lungs, not by the heart." This was almost word for word what Al-Nafis had written centuries earlier.

Harvey's Concern About the Church and His Aristotelian Concept of Circulation

There is no evidence that Harvey was aware of the Servetus book or Al-Nafis, but he was enrolled at the University of Padua in 1598 where Galileo was a tutor, and there is little doubt that he was highly influenced by Galileo's thinking. In 1616, Galileo was also persecuted and convicted of heresy for teaching that the earth revolved around the sun and was not the center of the universe. (It was not until 1992, almost 400 years later, that Galileo was officially vindicated by Pope John Paul II). Harvey, having announced his discovery the preceding year, prudently waited until 1628 to publish his book. His hesitation to openly defy Galen proved justified. Most physicians rejected his book because he could not explain how the arteries and veins met. If organs did not consume blood, how did different parts of the body obtain nourishment? If the liver did not make blood from food, where did blood originate? Why was blood blue in veins but red in arteries? It was over three decades before Harvey's achievements received proper acknowledgment. Another reason was that the discovery of capillaries, which were invisible even with the microscopes available at the time, was not made until 1642, by Marcello Malpighi, over two decades after Harvey's death.

Harvey never viewed the heart as a pump, but likened it to a bellows that lifted water by means of clacks (valves). "From the structure of the heart it is clear that the blood is constantly carried through the lungs into the aorta as by two clacks of a water bellows to raise water." This is the only mechanical analogy he ever offered, and was based on Aristotle's: "It is necessary to regard the structure of this organ [the lungs] as very similar to the sort of bellows used in a forge, for both lungs and heart take this form." Harvey's concept of circulation was also consistent with the Aristotelian view that it was cyclical (such as the apparent movements of celestial objects), rather than being perfectly circular. The example Aristotle gave was the cycle of the sun causing evaporation of water that condensed into clouds, then fell as rain, and was again evaporated. Thus Harvey writes in *De Motu Cordis*, "We have as much right to call the motion of the blood circular as Aristotle said that the air and rain emulate the circular movement of the heavenly bodies." It was the notion that as water gives life to land, so blood gives life to the body. Harvey needed this air-water-air analogy to explain the transfer of blood from arteries to veins, since capillaries had not yet been discovered.

There are numerous other reasons why the heart should not be viewed as a mere pump. An efficient pump would be designed to work directly on the system with the greatest volume, and the veins contain over five times more blood than the arteries (65% compared to 12%). The aorta bends during systole, when it should straighten under the higher pressure. More importantly, replacement by a mechanical pump only works for a limited time, in contrast to heart transplants, which can function normally for more than two decades. This became apparent in January 1985, when despite the adequate pumping of William Schroeder's artificial heart for over a month, his doctors reported that he had an "unusual excess of fluid retention" (around 30 lb) that could not be explained and was difficult to reduce. He had suffered one stroke and subsequently had two more that left him in a vegetative and bloated state for over a year, at which point he died from a lung infection. In a letter published in The New York Times entitled "Can an Artificial Heart Have its Reasons?" [Dr. Rosch's letter can be found at http://www.nytimes.com/1985/01/07/opinion/l-can-an-artificial-heart-have-its-reasons-194202.html -Ed.], I noted that the heart, in addition to being a pump, was also an exquisite endocrine organ that secreted powerful atrial natriuretic hormones that responded to excess fluid loads and lowered blood pressure faster and more profoundly than any known drugs. Deprived of this homeostatic mechanism, it was not surprising that Schroeder suffered an accumulation of excess fluid that his doctors said "could squash the blood vessels, slowing the circulation, thus increasing the chances for clots to form". Since that time, it has been found that the ventricles also secrete a similar blood pressure-reducing hormone, and that all four chambers of the heart can make and secrete oxytocin, the "bonding and cuddling" hormone.

Where Do Emotions Originate, and
Do We Have More Than One Mind or Brain?

The Ebers Papyrus suggests that as far back as 3000 B.C. the Egyptians considered mind and body to be inseparable. It included a treatise on the heart, which explained that the heart is the center of the blood supply, with vessels attached for every member of the body. The Chinese *Huangdi Neijing*, or Yellow Emperor's Classic of Internal Medicine, dated around 2500 B.C., similarly states, "The heart is the root of life and causes the versatility of the spiritual faculties." Aristotle and Virgil also taught that the heart, rather than the brain, was the seat of the mind and emotions. Harvey clearly recognized that the heart was much more than a mechanical pump, and reflected emotions and feelings, when he wrote, "Every affection of the mind that is attended either with pain or pleasure, hope or fear, is the cause of an agitation whose influence extends to the heart." His contemporary, the celebrated philosopher, scientist and mathematician René Descartes, respected Harvey and agreed that the blood circulated through the body in a closed system of arteries and veins contrary to Galen's teachings. But Descartes argued that the heart was not a pump, but a furnace. It heated small particles in the blood, causing them to expand, which forced the atrioventricular valves to close and opened the valves to the aorta and pulmonary artery. When the heated blood was released into the arteries, it caused them to expand, and when it cooled and took less space, the arteries and veins collapsed. It was the heated blood that animated the system rather than the heart.

Descartes viewed the human body as a complex machine, comparable to a complicated clock or the spectacular statues in French water gardens, that moved in response to changes in hydraulic pressure. Illness occurred when the body's machinery broke down and it was the physician's duty to find the source of the problem and repair it. As with most other machines, this could best be accomplished by gaining a better knowledge of the body's smallest working parts. Descartes also believed that man was unique because nothing else on earth had a mind or soul. In his *The Passions of the Soul*, he argued that like all other devices that produced motion, the machinery of the body obeyed the laws of physics. However, since mind/soul was a non-material and motionless gift from God, it was separate from the material mechanics of the body and not subject to any known laws. Mental disorders were also a mystery and beyond human comprehension. Like many other illnesses, they were often viewed as a punishment from God for some sin, or possibly even due to possession by an evil spirit that required exorcism. As a result, mental and emotional problems were more properly within the province of the Church, and should be treated by priests rather than physicians. For Descartes, the heart was simply part of the machinery of the body. It had nothing to do with the mind or soul. The latter he thought resided in the pineal gland—which he erroneously believed was found only in man, since other animals did not have souls—and connected the intellect with body. The pineal was also the connection between the mind and the heart, since if the heart was acting independently and not controlled by thought, it must have its own separate mind/soul.

Harvey was appalled at Descartes' purely mechanistic interpretation of his research. Others also disagreed with Descartes, especially with respect to emotions like love and faith in God. As the 17th-century mathematician and scientist Blaise Pascal wrote, "The heart has reasons that reason knows not of. We feel it in a thousand things . . . Do you love by reason? It is the heart which perceives God and not the reason. That is what faith is: God perceived by the heart, not by the reason." For Pascal, the heart was "the intuitive mind" rather than "the calculating (reasoning) mind". Where do emotions originate? William James proposed that an external stimulus leads to physiological responses and the resultant emotion depends upon how you interpret those responses: "The bodily changes follow directly the PERCEPTION of the exciting fact, and that our feeling of the same changes as they occur IS the emotion."

This theory was generally accepted until Walter Cannon showed that "fight or flight" responses to stress were due to stimulation of the sympathetic nervous system and secretion of hormones like adrenalin. If awareness of trembling, palpitations and other responses was what caused fear, then inducing these artificially in the absence of any threatening stimulus should have the same effect. But when he injected adrenalin into normal volunteers, although it produced the identical visceral responses, the subjects experienced no specific emotions. It was only when he discussed disturbing topics like sick children or their dead parents, and then injected adrenalin, that an emotion was induced. In another experiment, cats were kept alive and healthy after having their sympathetic nervous systems completely removed. However, this had little effect on their emotional responses. Cats displayed the typical signs of terror in response to a barking dog, while organs whose connections to the brain had not been completely destroyed reacted normally. In addition, the sympathetic nervous system's response to different emotional states such as fear and rage as well as stressors such as lack of oxygen and extremes of temperature is the same. If emotions resulted from these responses, one would expect fear and freezing to induce the same feelings, which is not the case.

With respect to whether feelings cause emotions or vice versa, subsequent theories have combined aspects of both or suggested they occur simultaneously but independently. The problem in evaluating these theories is the difficulty in defining exactly what constitutes an emotion, and how the term differs from others such as feelings, mood, affect, and temperament. The use of the word emotion dates back to the 16th century, when it was adapted from the French verb émouvoir, meaning "to stir up", and its derived noun émotion. This in turn dates back to the classical Latin phrase *motus anima*, to physically move out, or excite the spirit. "Emotion" was initially used only in its literal sense of physically moving or agitating something or someone, and it was not until the late 18th century that the meaning of "strong feeling" began to replace this.

In his 1649 *The Passions of the Soul*, Descartes wrote, "*The principle effect of the passions (emotions) is to move and dispose the soul to want the things for which they prepare the body. Thus the feeling of fear moves the soul to want to flee, that of courage to want to fight, and similarly with the others.*" Today, emotions are viewed as consistent responses to any internal or external event that has a particular significance for that specific individual. Feelings are best understood as a subjective representation of emotions that also differs for each of us. Moods are diffuse affective states that generally last for a longer period of time and are less intense than emotions. Affect is an encompassing term used to describe emotion, feelings, and moods together, although all of these are often used as synonyms. As illustrated above, there are similar semantic problems with mind, spirit and soul, which are also commonly used interchangeably, especially when translated from something written centuries ago in Greek, Latin, Arabic or French.

Even English words like mind and brain have become synonyms, although they are obviously quite different. The brain is a physical organ that can be seen and touched. It is located in the head, has a characteristic shape, and contains nerve cells and blood vessels. Specific areas of the brain have been shown to control seeing, hearing, talking, thinking, memory and various motor and sensory functions, and many believe that emotions originate or are stored in the brain, particularly the thalamus, amygdala and other components of the limbic system. In contrast, the mind is invisible, intangible and shapeless. It is responsible for attributes such as how we perceive things, how we know the difference between right and wrong, a firm and constant faith in some religious belief or healer, or why we love someone. Brain signals are transmitted via nervous system and humoral pathways, but we do not know how the mind communicates, and there is evidence that its location as well as that of the brain may not be limited to the confines of the skull. There is a "second brain", in the gut, that contains some 100 million neurons—more than in either the spinal cord or peripheral nerves. The gut's nervous system secretes 30 different neurotransmitters that affect the brain and other structures, and since 95% of the body's serotonin is found in the gut, it is no surprise that gastrointestinal complaints are the most common side effects of antidepressant drugs that inhibit serotonin metabolism. Irritable bowel syndrome, which may affect some 24 to 45 million Americans, is thought to be due in part to an excess of serotonin in the gut, and is regarded by some as a "mental illness" of this second brain.

The two brains have a common source and are intimately connected. During early fetal development, the esophagus, stomach, small intestine and colon, as well as the nervous system, develop from the same clump of embryonic tissue. When that divides, one section grows into the central nervous system (brain and cranial nerves) and the other into the enteric nervous system or "gut brain". During later stages the two brains become connected via the vagus, the largest of all the cranial nerves, but 90% of its fibers carry messages to the brain rather than the reverse. These may influence mood and emotions, and may explain why electrical stimulation of the vagus is FDA approved for treating drug resistant depression. Drugs like morphine and heroin also attach to the gut's opiate receptors, and the "gut brain" can become addicted to opiates. Our brain and gastrointestinal tract are so interconnected that both have natural 90-minute "sleep cycles". In the brain, slow-wave sleep is interrupted by periods of rapid eye movement (REM) during which dreams occur. The gut has corresponding 90-minute cycles of slow-wave muscle contractions, and as with the brain's REM

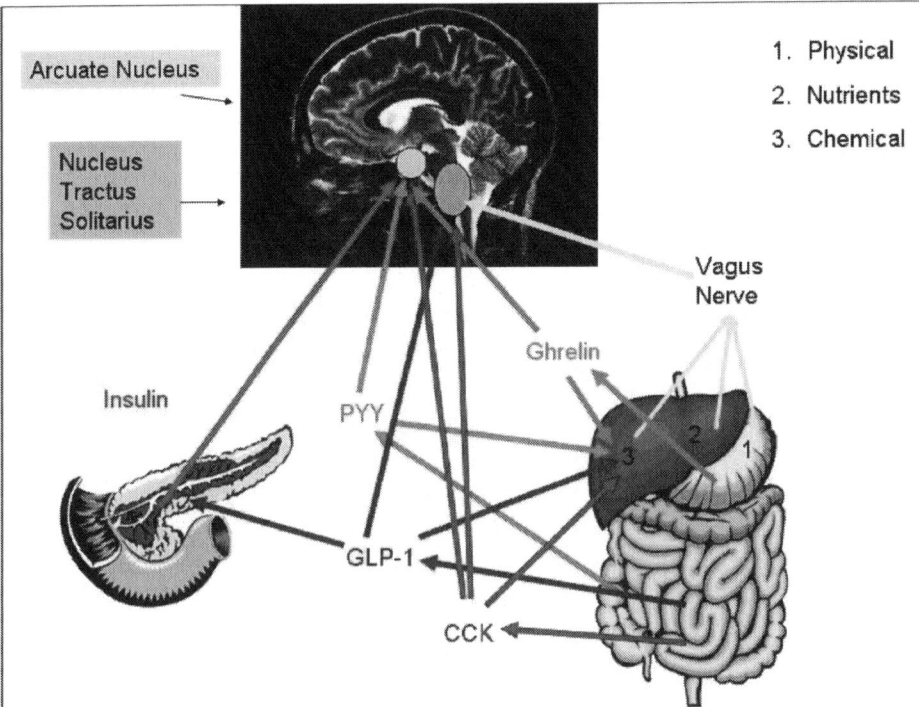

Gut–Brain Signaling Pathways: Proteins and hormones activate brain pathways in different ways, either by eventual vagal activation or through peripheral circulation. The nucleus tractus solitarii and the arcuate nucleus are then activated. Source: http://en.citizendium.org/wiki/Gut-brain_signalling

feel "butterflies" in the stomach prior to an important interview or examination. Since stress can also cause chronic indigestion, GERD, peptic ulcer, and spastic colon, "gut feelings" may be much more than a metaphor.

Researchers have also discovered a functional nervous system in the heart that is so sophisticated it is referred to as the "little brain". Its elaborate circuitry of neurons, support cells and neurotransmitters identical to those found in the cranial brain allows it to sense, learn, and remember on its own. The heart's "little brain" contains some 40,000 neurons that detect circulating hormones and neurochemicals and sense and respond to changes in heart rate and blood pressure. This information is transmitted to the medulla, which regulates autonomic nervous system activities, as well as higher brain centres that can influence perception, decision-making and other cognitive processes. In addition to nervous system connections, the heart can communicate with the brain through hormonal secretions and biophysical (pulse wave) signalling, as well as its powerful electromagnetic fields. Under normal circumstances, information is transmitted to and from the brain via afferent and efferent nerve fibers in the vagus and spinal column. These nerve connections are severed in a heart transplant and may never grow back. Nevertheless, a transplanted heart can function quite well independently for decades, possibly because its "little brain" has found alternate   communication pathways.

Do Emotions Come From the Heart and Body Rather Than the Head?

The early Egyptians certainly esteemed the heart and body. They reasoned that if the Nile and all vegetation could rise again, so could humans. Their elaborate embalming process was designed to preserve anything that might be needed in the next world or to facilitate resurrection. The abdominal organs were removed and placed in protective jars near the corpse, but the brain was discarded since it was considered useless. The only organ that was not removed was the heart, since it was believed to be the seat of the soul. Aristotle also viewed the heart as the site of the soul, rather than the brain, as well as the source of emotions and intelligence. He defined anger as a "seething heat in the region of the heart" along with "a desire for retaliation". While "brain" does not appear in the King James Bible, "heart" is mentioned almost 900 times, often in association with moods, emotions, or the ability to reason or think: "Why reason ye these things in your hearts?" (Mark 2:8). "Mind" is mentioned 96 times, and frequently in conjunction with heart—"which is in mine heart and in my mind" (1 Sam 2:35). "Love" appears 508 times in the Old Testament and 697 times in the New Testament, also often in conjunction with the heart: "And thou shalt love the Lᴏʀᴅ thy God with all thine heart, and with all thy soul, and with all thy might" (Deuteronomy 6:5). According to Buddha, "The way is not in the sky. The way is in the heart," and Shakespeare's King Henry IV said, "My crown is in my heart, not on my head."

Still today we use heart rather than brain to describe someone's emotions, mood, character or temperament, in expressions like heart of gold, cold-hearted, warm-hearted, downhearted, stouthearted, heavy-hearted, light-hearted, heartbroken or heartsick. We learn something by heart, get to the heart of things to find out what's really important, have a change of heart when we decide to go a different way, have a heart-to-heart talk to explain how we really feel and why, pour our heart out when we want to confess something, or take heart to have courage. Something from your "heart of hearts" reflects your sacred innermost feelings, or comes from your soul. The heart has long been the symbol of love—perhaps the most desirable emotion—which is why valentines are heart-shaped and red, the color of blood.

I began this explanation of why the heart is much more than a pump with some dictionary definitions that failed to acknowledge this. I intended to include the quotation "Where the heart lies, let the brain lie also" toward the end, and needed to its source. It was not under "heart" in Bartlett's *Familiar Quotations*, *The Oxford Dictionary of Quotations* or *Familiar Medical Quotations*. I eventually confirmed it was from "One Word More", a poem by Robert Browning dedicated to his wife; it was one of the more than 16,000 entries in *The International Thesaurus of Quotations*. What amazed and intrigued me was that although there were 1,067 topics in alphabetical order to choose from, some of which were obscure, there were no quotations under HEART, just this simple message: "See 282. EMOTIONS". Since this book was published in 1987, using *heart* and *emotions* as synonyms should not be considered a quaint or antiquated notion.

A New Paradigm of Energy Communication, and the Heart as "King of Organs"

The health of all living systems depends on good communication, both among constituents and with the external environment. We currently view communication via a chemical/molecular model, in which hormones and neurotransmitters fit into specific receptor sites on cell membranes like keys in a keyhole. However, humoral communication on such a random collision basis could never explain the myriad "fight or flight" responses to stress that occur simultaneously all over the body in milliseconds. In the final analysis, all communication takes place at a physical/atomic level via weak electrical signals from receptor sites that stimulate intracellular enzyme systems. EEG and ECG waves may not merely reflect the noise of the machinery of the brain and heart, but rather messages being sent to body sites that are tuned into them, much like a radio receives different messages depending on the transmitter station frequency it is tuned to receive. All living things have associated electromagnetic fields, and there is an emerging paradigm that posits illness as the result when these are disrupted. As illustrated in *Bioelectromagnetic and Subtle Energy Medicine*, due to be published later this year, correcting these abnormalities can result in remarkable improvement in patients with cardiomyopathy, metastatic cancer, drug resistant depression, Parkinson's, and other mental and degenerative neurological diseases. Doctors may soon be prescribing frequencies rather than pushing pills, because electromagnetic therapies are not only much safer, but also more cost effective.

The heart's electromagnetic field is estimated to be 5,000 times more powerful than the brain's. It permeates every cell in the body, and changes with different emotions. Since it extends several feet from the body, how you feel can affect someone who is nearby, especially if you are in physical contact with them, as noted below.

Women who work together for long periods of time also tend to have the same menstrual cycle, although this may be due to pheromones, and there may be other subtle energy communication mechanisms that have yet to be discovered. As previously emphasized, Arabic physicians have long considered the heart to be the most important organ in the body. They have also made significant contributions to our understanding of its role in circulation of the blood and human relationships hundreds of years before Harvey. And they are continuing to explore the mysteries of the heart and subtle energy communication in the biennial International Conference on Advanced Cardiac Sciences, founded in 2006 by Dr. Abdullah Al Abdulgader, Director of the Prince Sultan Cardiac Center, Hofuf, Saudi Arabia. I have been privileged to participate in and help organize the last three of these cutting-edge events, which—not surprisingly—are referred to as "The Heart, King of Organs Conference".

Dr. Paul J. Rosch, MD, MA, FACP, is Chairman of the Board of The American Institute of Stress, Clinical Professor of Medicine and Psychiatry at New York Medical College, Honorary Vice President of the International Stress Management Association and has served as Chair of its U.S. branch. He completed his internship and residency training at Johns Hopkins Hospital, and subsequently at the Walter Reed Army Hospital and Institute of Research, where he was Director of the Endocrine Section in the Department of Metabolism. He had a Fellowship at the Institute of Experimental Medicine and Surgery at the University of Montreal with Dr. Hans Selye, who originated the term "stress" as it is currently used, and has co-authored works with Dr. Selye as well as Dr. Flanders Dunbar, who introduced the term, "psychosomatic" into American medicine.

THE ENERGETIC HEART

BIOELECTROMAGNETIC INTERACTIONS WITHIN AND BETWEEN PEOPLE

Rollin McCraty

> Man's perceptions are not bounded by organs of perception;
> he perceives far more than sense (tho' ever so acute) can discover.
> —William Blake

The heart generates the largest electromagnetic field in the body. The electrical field as measured in an electrocardiogram (ECG) is about 60 times greater in amplitude than the brain waves recorded in an electroencephalogram (EEG). The magnetic component of the heart's field, which is around 5000 times stronger than that produced by the brain, is not impeded by tissues and can be measured several feet away from the body with Superconducting Quantum Interference Device (SQUID)-based magnetometers.[1] We have also found that the clear rhythmic patterns in beat-to-beat heart rate variability are distinctly altered when different emotions are experienced. These changes in electromagnetic, sound pressure, and blood pressure waves produced by cardiac rhythmic activity are "felt" by every cell in the body, further supporting the heart's role as a global internal synchronizing signal.

Biological Patterns Encode Information

One of the primary ways that signals and messages are encoded and transmitted in physiological systems is in the language of patterns. In the nervous system, it is well established that information is encoded in the time intervals between action potentials—patterns of electrical activity—and this may also

---

1   Stroink G. Principles of cardiomagnetism. In: Williamson SJ, Hoke M, Stroink G, Kotani M, eds. *Advances in Biomagnetism*. New York: Plenum Press, 1989:47-57.

apply to humoral communications. Several studies have revealed that biologically relevant information is encoded in the time interval between hormonal pulses[2,3,4]. As the heart secretes a number of different hormones with each contraction, there is a hormonal pulse pattern that correlates with heart rhythms. In addition to the encoding of information in the space between nerve impulses and in the intervals between hormonal pulses, it is likely that information is also encoded in the interbeat intervals of the pressure and electromagnetic waves produced by the heart. Karl Pribram has proposed that the low frequency oscillations generated by the heart and body in the form of afferent neural, hormonal, and electrical patterns are the carriers of emotional information, and that the higher frequency oscillations found in the EEG reflect the conscious perception and labelling of feelings and emotions[5].

Detecting Bioelectromagnetic Patterns Using Signal Averaging

A useful technique for detecting patterns in biological systems and investigating a number of bioelectromagnetic phenomena is signal averaging. This is accomplished by superimposing any number of equal-length epochs, each of which contains a repeating periodic signal. This emphasizes and distinguishes any signal that is time-locked to the periodic signal while eliminating variations that are not time-locked to the periodic signal. This procedure is commonly used to detect and record cerebral cortical responses to sensory stimulation[6]. When signal averaging is used to detect activity in the EEG that is time-locked to the ECG, the resultant waveform is called the heartbeat evoked potential.

---

2   Prank K, Schofl C, Laer L, Wagner M, von zur Muhlen A, Brabant G, Gabbiani F. Coding of time-varying hormonal signals in intracellular calcium spike trains. *Pac Symp Biocomput* 1998:633-644.

3   Schofl C, Prank K, Brabant G. Pulsatile hormone secretion for control of target organs. *Wien Med Wochenschr* 1995; 145:431-435.

4   Schofl C, Sanchez-Bueno A, Brabant G, Cobbold PH, Cuthbertson KS. Frequency and amplitude enhancement of calcium transients by cyclic AMP in hepatocytes. *Biochem J* 1991; 273:799-802.

5   Pribram K, Melges F. Psychophysiological basis of emotion. In: Vinken P, Bruyn G, eds. *Handbook of Clinical Neurology, Vol. 3*. Amsterdam: North-Holland Publishing Company, 1969:316-341.

6   Coles M, Gratton G, Fabini M. Event-related brain potentials. In: Cacioppo J, Tassinary L, eds. *Principles of Psychophysiology: Physical, Social and Inferential Elements*. New York: Cambridge University Press, 1990.

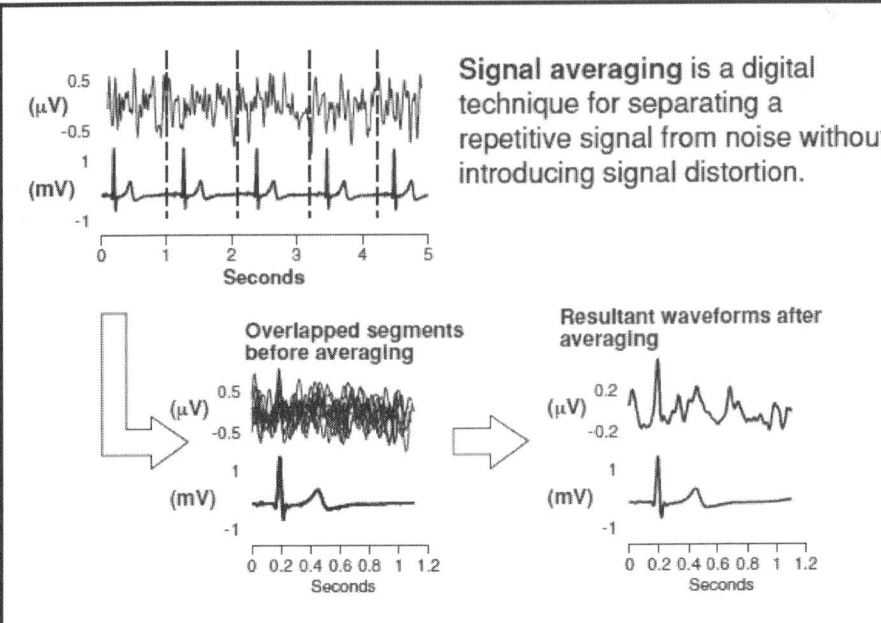

Signal averaging is a digital technique for separating a repetitive signal from noise without introducing signal distortion.

Figure 1. Signal averaging.

The sequence of the signal averaging procedure is shown above. First, the signals recorded from the EEG and ECG are digitized and stored in a computer. The R-wave (peak) of the ECG is used as the time reference for cutting the EEG and ECG signals into individual segments. The individual segments are then averaged together to produce the resultant waveforms. Only signals that are repeatedly synchronous with the ECG are present in the resulting waveform. Signals not related to the signal source (ECG) are eliminated through this process.

The Heartbeat Evoked Potential

In looking at heartbeat evoked potential data, it can be seen that the electromagnetic signal arrives at the brain instantaneously, while a host of different neural signals reach the brain starting about 8 milliseconds later and continue arriving throughout the cardiac cycle. Although the precise timing varies with each cycle, at around 240 milliseconds the blood pressure wave arrives at the brain and acts to synchronize neural activity, especially the alpha rhythm. It is also possible that information is encoded in the shape (modulation) of the ECG wave itself. For example, if one examines consecutive ECG cycles, it can be seen that each wave is slightly varied in a complex manner.

As indicated, the heart generates a powerful pressure wave that travels rapidly throughout the arteries much faster than the actual flow of blood that we feel as our pulse. These pressure waves force the blood cells through the capillaries to provide oxygen and nutrients to cells and expand the arteries, causing them to generate a relatively large electrical voltage. These waves also apply pressure to the cells in a rhythmic fashion that can cause some of their proteins to generate an electrical current in response to this "squeeze." Experiments conducted in our laboratory have shown that a change in the brain's electrical activity can be seen when the blood pressure wave reaches the brain around 240 milliseconds after systole.

There is a replicable and complex distribution of heartbeat evoked potentials across the scalp. Changes in these evoked potentials associated with the heart's afferent neurological input to the brain are detectable between 50 to 550 milliseconds after the heartbeat[7]. Gary Schwartz and colleagues at the University of Arizona believe the earlier components in this complex distribution cannot be explained by simple physiological mechanisms alone and suggest that an energetic interaction between the heart and brain also occurs[8]. They have confirmed our findings that heart-focused attention is associated with increased heart-brain synchrony, providing further support for energetic heart-brain communications. Schwartz and colleagues also demonstrated that when subjects focused their attention on the perception of their heartbeat, the synchrony in the preventricular region of the heartbeat evoked potential increased. From this they concluded that preventricular synchrony may reflect an energetic mechanism of heart-brain communication, while postventricular synchrony most likely reflects direct physiological mechanisms.[8]

The Heart's Role in Emotion

Throughout the 1990s, the view that the brain and body work in conjunction in order for perceptions, thoughts, and emotions to emerge gained momentum and is now widely accepted. The brain is an analog processor that relates whole concepts (patterns) to one another and looks for similarities, differences, or relationships between them, in contrast to a digital computer that assembles thoughts and feelings from bits of data. This new understanding of how the

7   Schandry R, Montoya P. Event-related brain potentials and the processing of cardiac activity. *Biol Psychol* 1996; 42:75-85.

8   Song L, Schwartz G, Russek L. Heart-focused attention and heart-brain synchronization: Energetic and physiological mechanisms. *Altern Ther Health Med* 1998; 4:44-62.

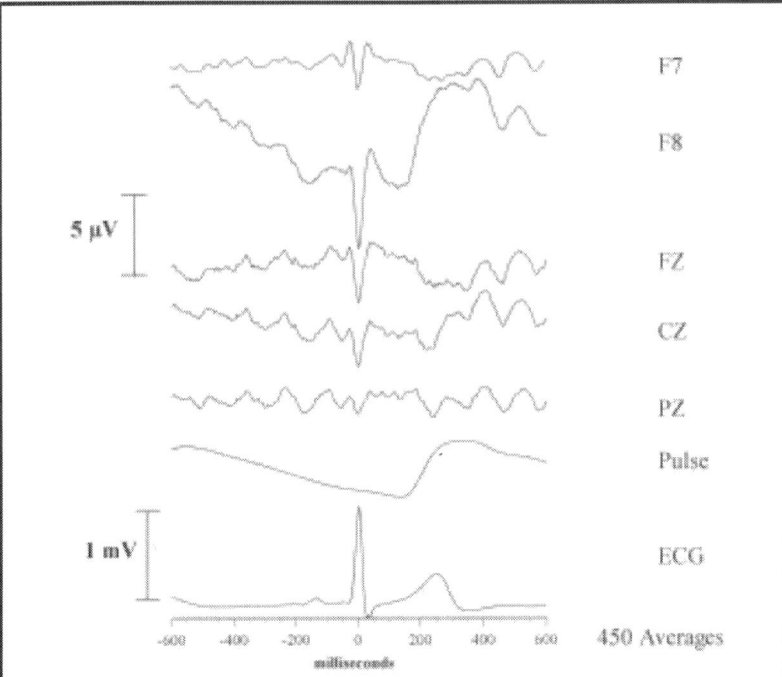

Figure 2. Heartbeat evoked potentials.
This figure shows an example of typical heartbeat evoked potentials. In this example, 450 averages were used. The pulse wave is also shown, indicating the timing relationship of the blood pressure wave reaching the brain. In this example, there is less synchronized alpha activity immediately after the R-wave. The time range between 10 and 250 milliseconds is when afferent signals from the heart are impinging upon the brain, and the alpha desynchronization indicates the processing of this information. Increased alpha activity can be clearly seen later in the waveforms, starting at around the time the blood pressure wave reaches the brain.

brain functions has challenged several long-standing assumptions about the nature of emotions. While it was formerly maintained that emotions originated only in the brain, we now recognize that emotions can be more accurately described as a product of the brain and body acting in concert. Moreover, evidence suggests that of the bodily organs, the heart may play a particularly important role in emotional experience. Research in the relatively new discipline of neurocardiology has confirmed that the heart is a sensory organ and acts as a sophisticated information encoding and processing center that enables it to learn, remember, and make independent functional decisions that do not involve the cerebral cortex[9]. Additionally, numerous experiments have demonstrated that patterns of cardiac afferent neurological input to the brain not only affect autonomic regulatory centers, but also influence higher brain centers involved in perception and emotional processing[10,11,12,13].

Heart rate variability (HRV), derived from the ECG, is a measure of the naturally occurring beat-to-beat changes in heart rate that has proven to be invaluable in studying the physiology of emotions. The analysis of HRV, or heart rhythms, provides a powerful, non-invasive measure of neurocardiac function that reflects heart-brain interactions and autonomic nervous system dynamics, which are particularly sensitive to changes in emotional states[14,15]. Our research, along with that of others, suggests that there is an important link between emotions and changes in the patterns of both efferent (descending) and afferent (ascending) autonomic activity[12,14,16,1718]. These changes in autonomic activity are associated with dramatic changes in the pattern of the heart's rhythm that often occur without any change in the amount of heart rate variability. Specifically, we have found that during the experience of negative emotions such as anger,

---

9 Armour J, Ardell J. *Neurocardiology*. New York: Oxford University Press, 1994.

10 Sandman CA, Walker BB, Berka C. Influence of afferent cardiovascular feedback on behavior and the cortical evoked potential. In: Cacioppo JT, Petty RE, eds. *Perspectives in Cardiovascular Psychophysiology*. New York: The Guilford Press, 1982:189-222.

11 Frysinger RC, Harper RM. Cardiac and respiratory correlations with unit discharge in epileptic human temporal lobe. *Epilepsia* 1990; 31:162-171.

12 McCraty R. Heart-brain neurodynamics: The making of emotions. In: Childre D, McCraty R, Wilson BC, eds. *Emotional Sovereignty*. Amsterdam: Harwood Academic Publishers.

13 van der Molen M, Somsen R, Orlebeke J. The rhythm of the heart beat in information processing. In: Ackles P, Jennings JR, Coles M, eds. *Advances in Psychophysiology, Vol. 1*. London: JAI Press, 1985:1-88.

14 Tiller W, McCraty R, Atkinson M. Cardiac coherence: A new, noninvasive measure of autonomic nervous system order. *Altern Ther Health Med* 1996; 2:52-65.

15 McCraty R, Singer D. Heart rate variability: A measure of autonomic balance and physiological coherence. In: Childre D, McCraty R, Wilson BC, eds. *Emotional Sovereignty*. Amsterdam: Harwood Academic Publishers.

16 McCraty R, Atkinson M, Tiller WA, Rein G, Watkins A. The effects of emotions on short term heart rate variability using power spectrum analysis. *Am J Cardiol* 1995; 76:1089-1093.

17 McCraty R, Barrios-Choplin B, Rozman D, Atkinson M, Watkins A. The impact of a new emotional self-management program on stress, emotions, heart rate variability, DHEA and cortisol. *Integr Physiol Behav Sci* 1998; 33:151-170.

18 Collet C, Vernet-Maury E, Delhomme G, Dittmar A. Autonomic nervous system response patterns specificity to basic emotions. *J Auton Nerv Sys* 1997; 62:45-57.

frustration, or anxiety, heart rhythms become more erratic and disordered, indicating less synchronization in the reciprocal action that ensues between the parasympathetic and sympathetic branches of the autonomic nervous system (ANS).[14,16] In contrast, sustained positive emotions, such as appreciation, love, or compassion, are associated with highly ordered or coherent patterns in the heart rhythms, reflecting greater synchronization between the two branches of the ANS, and a shift in autonomic balance toward increased parasympathetic activity[14, 16, 17, 19] (Figure 3).

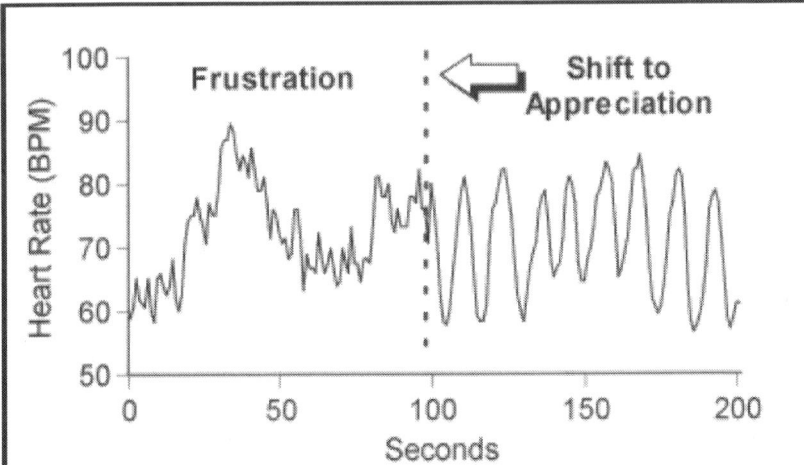

Figure 3. Emotions are reflected in heart rhythm patterns.
Real-time heart rate variability (heart rhythm) pattern of an individual making an intentional shift from a self-induced state of frustration to a genuine feeling of appreciation by using a positive emotion refocusing exercise known as the Freeze-Frame technique. It is of note that when the recording is analyzed statistically, the amount of heart rate variability is found to remain virtually the same during the two different emotional states; however, the pattern of the heart rhythm changes distinctly. Note the immediate shift from an erratic, disordered heart rhythm pattern associated with frustration to a smooth, harmonious, sine wave-like (coherent) pattern as the individual uses the positive emotion refocusing technique and self-generates a heartfelt feeling of appreciation.

19   McCraty R, Atkinson M, Tomasino D, Goelitz J, Mayrovitz H. The impact of an emotional self-management skills course on psychosocial functioning and autonomic recovery to stress in middle school children. *Integr Physiol Behav Sci* 1999; 34:246-268.

Physiological Coherence

Based on these findings, we have introduced the term physiological coherence to describe a number of related physiological phenomena associated with more ordered and harmonious interactions among the body's systems[20].

The term coherence has several related definitions. A common definition of the term is "the quality of being logically integrated, consistent, and intelligible," as in a coherent argument. In this context, thoughts and emotional states can be considered "coherent" or "incoherent." Importantly, however, these associations are not merely metaphorical, as different emotions are in fact associated with different degrees of coherence in the oscillatory rhythms generated by the body's various systems.

The term "coherence" is used in physics to describe the ordered or constructive distribution of power within a waveform. The more stable the frequency and shape of the waveform, the higher the coherence. An example of a coherent wave is the sine wave. The term autocoherence is used to denote this kind of coherence. In physiological systems, this type of coherence describes the degree of order and stability in the rhythmic activity generated by a single oscillatory system. Methodology for computing coherence has been published elsewhere.[14]

Coherence also describes two or more waves that are either phase- or frequency-locked. In physiology, coherence is used to describe a functional mode in which two or more of the body's oscillatory systems, such as respiration and heart rhythms, become entrained and oscillate at the same frequency. The term cross-coherence is used to specify this type of coherence.

All the above definitions apply to the study of both emotional physiology and bioelectromagnetism. We have found that positive emotions are associated with a higher degree of coherence within the heart's rhythmic activity (autocoherence) as well as increased coherence between different oscillatory systems (cross-coherence/entrainment).[14, 20] Typically, entrainment is observed between heart rhythms, respiratory rhythms, and blood pressure oscillations; however, other biological oscillators, including very low frequency brain rhythms, craniosacral rhythms, electrical potentials measured across the skin, and, most likely, rhythms in the digestive system, can also become entrained.[20]

We have also demonstrated that physiological coherence is associated with increased synchronization between the heartbeat (ECG) and alpha rhythms in the EEG. In experiments measuring heartbeat evoked potentials, we found that

---

20   McCraty R, Atkinson M. Psychophysiological coherence. In: Childre D, McCraty R, Wilson BC, eds. *Emotional Sovereignty*. Amsterdam: Harwood Academic Publishers.

the brain's alpha activity (8-12 hertz frequency range) is naturally synchronized to the cardiac cycle. However, when subjects used a positive emotion refocusing technique to consciously self-generate feelings of appreciation, their heart rhythm coherence significantly increased, as did the ratio of the alpha rhythm that was synchronized to the heart.[20, 21]

Another related phenomenon associated with physiological coherence is resonance. In physics, resonance refers to a phenomenon whereby an unusually large vibration is produced in a system in response to a stimulus whose frequency is identical or nearly identical to the natural vibratory frequency of the system. The frequency of the vibration produced in such a state is said to be the resonant frequency of the system. When the human system is operating in the coherent mode, increased synchronization occurs between the sympathetic and parasympathetic branches of the ANS, and entrainment between the heart rhythms, respiration and blood pressure oscillations is observed. This occurs because these oscillatory subsystems are all vibrating at the resonant frequency of the system. Most models show that the resonant frequency of the human cardio-vascular system is determined by the feedback loops between the heart and brain[22,23]. In humans and in many animals, the resonant frequency is approximately 0.1 hertz, which is equivalent to a 10-second rhythm.

In summary, we use coherence as an umbrella term to describe a physiological mode that encompasses entrainment, resonance, and synchronization—distinct but related phenomena, all of which emerge from the harmonious activity and interactions of the body's subsystems. Correlates of physiological coherence include: increased synchronization between the two branches of the ANS, a shift in autonomic balance toward increased parasympathetic activity, increased heart-brain synchronization, increased vascular resonance, and entrainment between diverse physiological oscillatory systems. The coherent mode is reflected by a smooth, sine wave-like pattern in the heart rhythms (heart rhythm coherence) and a narrow-band, high-amplitude peak in the low frequency range of the heart rate variability power spectrum, at a frequency of about 0.1 hertz.

21   McCraty R. Influence of cardiac afferent input on heartbrain synchronization and cognitive performance. *Int J Psychophysiol* 2002; 45:72-73.

22   Baselli G, Cerutti S, Badilini F, Biancardi L, Porta A, Pagani M, Lombardi F, Rimoldi O, Furlan R, Malliani A. Model for the assessment of heart period variability interactions of respiration influences. *Med Biol Eng Comput* 1994; 32:143-152.

23   deBoer RW, Karemaker JM, Strackee J. Hemodynamic fluctuations and baroreflex sensitivity in humans: A beatto-beat model. *Am J Physiol* 1987; 253:H680-H689.

Benefits of Coherence

Coherence confers a number of benefits to the system in terms of both physiological and psychological functioning. At the physiological level, there is increased efficiency in fluid exchange, filtration, and absorption between the capillaries and tissues; increased ability of the cardiovascular system to adapt to circulatory demands; and increased temporal synchronization of cells throughout the body[24,25]. This results in increased system-wide energy efficiency and conservation of metabolic energy. These observations support the link between positive emotions and increased physiological efficiency that may partially explain the growing number of documented correlations between positive emotions, improved health, and increased longevity[26,27,28]. We have also shown that practicing certain techniques that increase physiological coherence is associated with both short-term and long-term improvement in several objective health-related measures, including enhanced humoral immunity[29,30] and an increased DHEA/cortisol ratio.[17]

Increased physiological coherence is similarly associated with psychological benefits, including improvements in cognitive performance and mental clarity as well as increased emotional stability and well-being.[20,31] Studies conducted in diverse populations have documented significant reductions in stress and negative affect and increases in positive mood and attitudes in individuals using

24   Langhorst P, Schulz G, Lambertz M. Oscillating neuronal network of the "common brainstem system." In: Miyakawa K, Koepchen H, Polosa C, eds. *Mechanisms of Blood Pressure Waves*. Tokyo: Japan Scientific Societies Press, 1984:257-275.

25   Siegel G, Ebeling BJ, Hofer HW, Nolte J, Roedel H, Klubendorf D. Vascular smooth muscle rhythmicity. In: Miyakawa K, Koepchen H, Polosa C, eds. *Mechanisms of Blood Pressure Waves*. Tokyo: Japan Scientific Societies Press, 1984:319-338.

26   Danner DD, Snowdon DA, Friesen WV. Positive emotions in early life and longevity: Findings from the nun study. *J Pers Soc Psychol* 2001; 80:804-813.

27   Salovey P, Rothman A, Detweiler J, Steward W. Emotional states and physical health. *Am Psychol* 2000; 55:110-121.

28   Russek LG, Schwartz GE. Feelings of parental caring predict health status in midlife: A 35-year follow-up of the Harvard Mastery of Stress Study. *J Behav Med* 1997; 20:1-13.

29   Rein G, Atkinson M, McCraty R. The physiological and psychological effects of compassion and anger. *J Adv Med* 1995; 8:87-105.

30   McCraty R, Atkinson M, Rein G, Watkins AD. Music enhances the effect of positive emotional states on salivary IgA. *Stress Med* 1996; 12:167-175.

31   McCraty R, Atkinson M, Tomasino D. *Science of the Heart*. Boulder Creek, CA: HeartMath Research Center, Institute of HeartMath, Publication No. 01-001, 2001.

Victoria is a pseudonym. The client is not recognizable from the text and has given her informed consent.

coherence-building techniques.[17, 19, 29, 31,32]

Improvements in clinical status, emotional well-being and quality of life have also been demonstrated in various medical patient populations in intervention programs using coherence-building approaches. For example, significant blood pressure reductions have been demonstrated in individuals with hypertension;[33] improved functional capacity and reduced depression in congestive heart failure patients;[34] improved psychological health and quality of life in patients with diabetes;[35] and improvements in asthma.[36] Another study reported reductions in pathological symptoms and anxiety and significant improvements in positive affect, physical vitality, and general well-being in individuals with HIV infection and AIDS.[37]

Additionally, patient case history data provided by numerous health care professionals report substantial improvements in health and psychological status and frequent reductions in medication requirements in patients with such medical conditions as cardiac arrhythmias, chronic fatigue, environmental sensitivity, fibromyalgia, and chronic pain.[38] Finally, techniques that increase physiological coherence have been used effectively by mental health professionals in the treatment of emotional disorders, including anxiety, depression, panic disorder, and post-traumatic stress disorder.[38]

32   Barrios-Choplin B, McCraty R, Cryer B. An inner quality approach to reducing stress and improving physical and emotional wellbeing at work. *Stress Med* 1997; 13:193-201.

33   McCraty R, Atkinson M, Tomasino D. Impact of a workplace stress reduction program on blood pressure and emotional health in hypertensive employees. *J Altern Complement Med*. 2003 Jun; 9(3):355-69.

34   Luskin F, Reitz M, Newell K, Quinn TG, Haskell W. A controlled pilot study of stress management training of elderly patients with congestive heart failure. *Prev Cardiol* 2002; 5:168-172, 176.

35   McCraty R, Atkinson M, Lipsenthal L. Emotional selfregulation program enhances psychological health and quality of life in patients with diabetes. Boulder Creek, CA: HeartMath Research Center, Institute of HeartMath, Publication No. 00-006, 2000.

36   Lehrer P, Smetankin A, Potapova T. Respiratory sinus arrhythmia biofeedback therapy for asthma: A report of 20 unmedicated pediatric cases. *Appl Psychophysiol Biofeedback* 2000; 25:193-200.

37   Rozman D, Whitaker R, Beckman T, Jones D. A pilot intervention program which reduces psychological symptomatology in individuals with human immunodeficiency virus. *Complemen Ther Med* 1996; 4:226-232.

38   McCraty R, Tomasino D, Atkinson M. Research, clinical perspectives, and case histories. In: Childre D, McCraty R, Wilson BC, eds. *Emotional Sovereignty*. Amsterdam: Harwood Academic Publishers

Drivers of Physiological Coherence

Although physiological coherence is a natural state that can occur sponta-neously during sleep and deep relaxation, sustained episodes during normal daily activities are generally rare. While specific rhythmic breathing methods can induce coherence for brief periods, cognitively directed, paced breathing is difficult for many people to maintain. On the other hand, our findings indi-cate that individuals can produce extended periods of physiological coherence by actively generating and sustaining a feeling of appreciation or other posi-tive emotions. Sincere positive feelings appear to excite the system at its reso-nant frequency, allowing the coherent mode to emerge naturally. This typically makes it easier for people to sustain a positive emotion for much longer periods, thus facilitating the process of establishing and reinforcing coherent patterns in the neural architecture as the familiar reference. Once a new pattern is es-tablished, the brain strives to maintain a match with the new program, thus increasing the probability of maintaining coherence and reducing stress, even during challenging situations.[12]

Doc Childre, founder of the Institute of Heart-Math, has developed a num-ber of practical positive emotion refocusing and emotional restructuring tech-niques that allow people to quickly self-generate coherence at will.[39,40] Known as the HeartMath system, these techniques utilize the heart as a point of entry into the psychophysiological networks that connect the physiological, mental, and emotional systems. In essence, because the heart is a primary generator of rhythmic neural and energetic patterns in the body—influencing brain process-es that control the ANS, cognitive function and emotion—it provides an access point from which system-wide dynamics can be quickly and profoundly affect-ed. Research studies and the experience of numerous health care professionals indicate that HeartMath coherence-building techniques are easily learned, have a high rate of compliance, and are highly adaptable to a wide range of demo-graphic groups.

39   Childre D, Martin H. *The HeartMath Solution*. San Francisco: HarperSanFrancis-co, 1999.

40   Childre D, Rozman, D. *Overcoming Emotional Chaos: Eliminate Anxiety, Lift De-pression and Create Security in Your Life*. San Diego: Jodere Group, 2002.

Promoting Physiological Coherence Through Heart Rhythm Coherence Feedback Training

Used in conjunction with positive emotion-based coherence-building techniques, heart rhythm feedback training can be a powerful tool to assist people in learning how to self-generate increased physiological coherence.[41] We have developed a portable heart rhythm monitoring and feedback system that enables physiological coherence to be objectively monitored and quantified. Known as the emWave system (HeartMath LLC, Boulder Creek, CA), this interactive hardware/software system monitors and displays individuals' heart rate variability patterns in real time as they practice the positive emotion refocusing and emotional restructuring techniques taught in the integrated package. Using a sensor to record the pulse wave, the system plots changes in heart rate on a beat-to-beat basis. As people practice the coherence-building techniques, they can readily see and experience the changes in their heart rhythm patterns, which generally become more ordered, smoother, and more sine wave-like as they experience positive emotions. This process reinforces the natural association between the physiological coherence mode and positive feelings. The software also analyzes the heart rhythm patterns for coherence level, which is fed back to the user as an accumulated numerical score or success in playing one of three on-screen games designed to reinforce the coherence-building skills. The real-time physiological feedback essentially takes the guesswork and randomness out of the process of self-inducing a coherent state, resulting in greater consistency, focus, and effectiveness in shifting to a beneficial psychophysiological mode.

Heart rhythm coherence feedback training has been successfully used in clinical settings by physicians, mental health professionals and neurofeedback therapists to facilitate health improvements in patients with numerous physical and psychological disorders. It is also increasingly being utilized in corporate, law enforcement, and educational settings to enhance physical and emotional health and improve performance.

Heart Rhythms and Bioelectromagnetism

The first biomagnetic signal was demonstrated in 1963 by Gerhard Baule and Richard McFee in a magnetocardiogram (MCG) that used magnetic induction

---

41   McCraty R. Heart rhythm coherence – An emerging areaof biofeedback. *Biofeedback* 2002; 30:17-19.

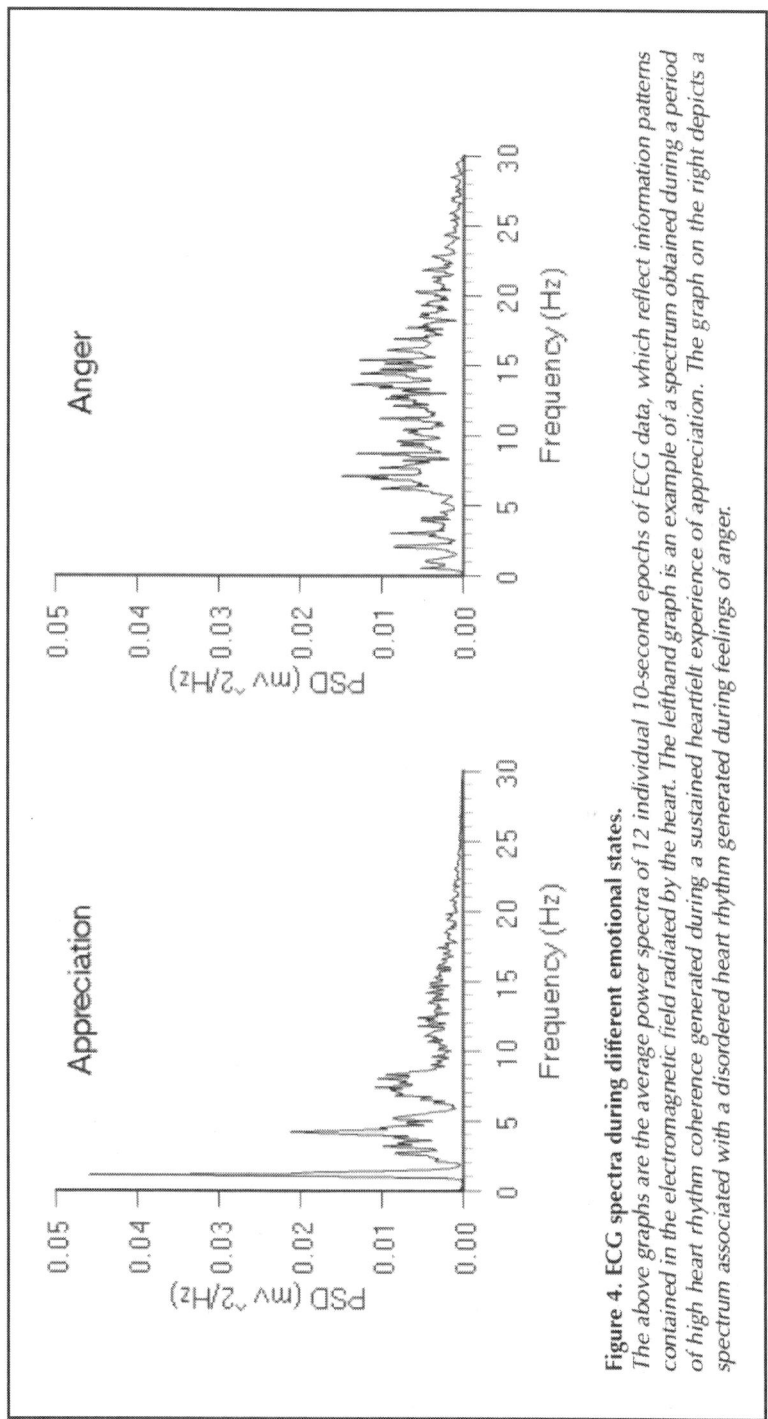

Figure 4. ECG spectra during different emotional states.
The above graphs are the average power spectra of 12 individual 10-second epochs of ECG data, which reflect information patterns contained in the electromagnetic field radiated by the heart. The lefthand graph is an example of a spectrum obtained during a period of high heart rhythm coherence generated during a sustained heartfelt experience of appreciation. The graph on the right depicts a spectrum associated with a disordered heart rhythm generated during feelings of anger.

coils to detect fields generated by the human heart.[42] A remarkable increase in the sensitivity of biomagnetic measurements was achieved with the introduction of the Superconducting Quantum Interference Device (SQUID) in the early 1970s, and the ECG and MCG have since been shown to closely parallel one another.[43]

The heart generates a series of electromagnetic pulses in which the time interval between each beat varies in a complex manner. These pulsing waves of electromagnetic energy create fields within fields and give rise to interference patterns when they interact with magnetically polarizable tissues and substances.

Figure 4 shows two different power spectra derived from an average of 12 individual 10-second epochs of ECG data recorded during differing psychophysiological modes. The plot on the left was produced while the subject was in a state of deep appreciation, whereas the plot on the right was generated while the subject experienced recalled feelings of anger. The difference in the patterns, and thus the information they contain, can be clearly seen. There is a direct correlation between the patterns in the heart rate variability rhythm and the frequency patterns in the spectrum of the ECG or MCG. Experiments such as these indicate that psychophysiological information can be encoded into the electromagnetic fields produced by the heart.[14,44]

Bioelectromagnetic Communication Between People

The human body is replete with mechanisms for detecting its external environment. Sense organs, the most obvious example, are specifically geared to react to touch, temperature, select ranges of light and sound waves, etc. These organs are acutely sensitive to external stimuli. The nose, for example, can detect one molecule of gas, while a cell in the retina of the eye can detect a single photon of light; and if the ear were any more sensitive, it would pick up the sound of the random vibrations of its own molecules.[45]

The interaction between two human beings— for example, the consultation between a patient and her clinician—is a very sophisticated dance that involves many subtle factors. Most people tend to think of communication solely in

42   Baule G, McFee R. Detection of the magnetic field of the heart. *Am Heart J* 1963; 55:95-96.

43   Nakaya Y. Magnetocardiography: A comparison with electrocardiography. *J Cardiogr Suppl* 1984; 3:31-40.

44   McCraty R, Atkinson M, Tiller WA. New electrophysiological correlates associated with intentional heart focus. *Subtle Energies* 1993; 4:251-268.

45   Russell P. *The Brain Book*. New York: Penguin Books USA, 1979.

terms of overt signals expressed through facial movements, voice qualities, gestures and body movements. However, evidence now supports the perspective that a subtle yet influential electromagnetic or "energetic" communication system operates just below our conscious level of awareness. The following section will discuss data suggesting that this energetic system contributes to the "magnetic" attractions or repulsions that occur between individuals. It is also quite possible that these energetic interactions can affect the therapeutic process.

The concept of energy or information exchange between individuals is central to many of the Eastern healing arts, but its acceptance in Western medicine has been hampered by the lack of a plausible mechanism to explain the nature of this "energy information" or how it is communicated. However, numerous studies investigating the effects of healers, Therapeutic Touch practitioners, and other individuals have demonstrated a wide range of significant effects including the influence of "energetic" approaches on wound healing rates,[46,47] pain,[48,49] haemoglobin levels,[50] conformational changes of DNA and water structure,[51,52] as well as psychological states.[53] Although these reports show beneficial results, they have been largely ignored because of the lack of any scientific rationale to explain how the effects are achieved.

Physiological Linkage and Empathy

The ability to sense what other people are feeling is an important factor in allowing us to connect or communicate effectively with others. The smoothness or flow in any social interaction depends to a great extent on the establishment

46   Wirth DP. The effect of non-contact therapeutic touch on the healing rate of full thickness dermal wounds. *Subtle Energies* 1990; 1:1-20.

47   Grad B. Some biological effects of the laying on of hands: Review of experiments with animals and plants. *J Am Soc Psychical Res* 1965; 59:95-171.

48   Keller E. Effects of therapeutic touch on tension headache pain. *Nurs Res* 1986; 35:101-105.

49   Redner R, Briner B, Snellman L. Effects of a bioenergy healing technique on chronic pain. *Subtle Energies* 1991; 2:43-68.

50   Krieger D. Healing by the laying on of hands as a facilitator of bioenergetic change: The response of in-vivo human hemoglobin. *Psychoenerg Syst* 1974; 1:121-129.

51   Rein G, McCraty R. Structural changes in water and DNA associated with new physiologically measurable states. *J Sci Explor* 1994; 8:438-439.

52   Rein G, McCraty R. Modulation of DNA by coherent heart frequencies. *Proceedings of the Third Annual Conference of the International Society for the Study of Subtle Energy and Energy Medicine,* Monterey, CA, June 25-29, 1993:58-62.

53   Quinn J. Therapeutic touch as an energy exchange: Testing the theory. ANS Adv Nurs Sci 1984; 6:42-49.

of a spontaneous entrainment or linkage between individuals. When people are engaged in deep conversation, they begin to fall into a subtle dance, synchronizing their movements and postures, vocal pitch, speaking rates, and length of pauses between responses,[54] and, as we are now discovering, important aspects of their physiology can also become linked and entrained.

Several studies have investigated different types of physiological synchronization or entrainment between individuals during empathetic moments or between clinician and patient during therapeutic sessions. One study by Levenson and Gottman at the University of California at Berkeley looked at physiological synchronization in married couples during empathetic interactions. Researchers examined couples' physiological responses during two discussions: a neutral "How was your day?" conversation, to establish a baseline, and a second conversation containing more emotional content in which the couples were asked to spend fifteen minutes discussing something about which they disagreed. After the disagreement, one partner was asked to leave the room while the other stayed to watch a replay of the talk and identify portions of the dialogue where he or she was actually empathizing but did not express it. Both spouses individually engaged in this procedure. Levenson was then able to identify those segments of the video where empathy occurred and match the empathetic response to physiological responses in both partners. He found that in partners who were adept at empathizing, their physiology mimicked their partner's while they empathized. If the heart rate of one went up, so did the heart rate of the other; if the heart rate slowed, so did that of the empathic spouse.[55] Other studies observing the psychophysiology of married couples while interacting were able to predict the probability of divorce.[56]

Although studies that have examined physiological linkages between therapists and patients have suffered from methodological challenges, they do support a tendency to autonomic attunement during periods of empathy between the therapist and patient.[57] Dana Redington, a psychophysiologist at the University of California, San Francisco, analyzed heart rate variability patterns during therapist-patient interactions using a non-linear dynamics approach. Redington and colleagues used phase space maps to plot changes in the beat-to-beat heart rate of both the therapist and patient during psychotherapy sessions. They found that the trajectories in the therapist's patterns often coincided with

---

54   Hatfield E. *Emotional Contagion*. New York: Cambridge University Press, 1994.

55   Levenson RW, Ruef AM. Physiological aspects of emotional knowledge and rapport. In: Ickes W, ed. *Empathic Accuracy*. New York: Guilford Press, 1997.

56   Levenson R, Gottman J. Physiological and affective predictors of change in relationship satisfaction. *J Pers Soc Psychol* 1985; 49:85-94.

57   Robinson J, Herman A, Kaplan B. Autonomic responses correlate with counselor-client empathy. *J Couns Psychol* 1982; 29:195-198.

the patient's during moments when the therapist experienced strong feelings of empathy for the patient.[58] Carl Marci at Harvard University found evidence of a more direct linkage between patients and therapists using skin conductance measures. During sessions of psychodynamic psychotherapy, Marci observed a quantifiable fluctuation and entrainment in the pattern of physiological linkage within patient-therapist dyads, which was related to patient perception of the therapist's empathy. In addition, the preliminary results of his studies indicate that during periods of low physiological linkage there are fewer empathetic comments, more incidents of incorrect interpretations, less shared affect, and fewer shared behavioral responses when compared to episodes of high physiological linkage.[59]59

Cardioelectromagnetic Communication

An important step in testing our hypothesis that the heart's electromagnetic field could transmit signals between people was to determine if the field and the information modulated within it could be detected by other individuals.

In conducting these experiments, the question being asked was straightforward. Namely, can the electromagnetic field generated by the heart of one individual be detected in physiologically relevant ways in another person, and if so does it have any discernible biological effects? To investigate these possibilities, we used signal-averaging techniques to detect signals that were synchronous with the peak of the R-wave of one subject's ECG in recordings of another subject's electroencephalogram (EEG) or brain waves. My colleagues and I have performed numerous experiments in our laboratory over a period of several years using these techniques,[60] and several examples are included below to illustrate some of these findings. In the majority of these experiments, subjects were seated in comfortable, high-back chairs to minimize postural changes with the positive ECG electrode located on the side at the left sixth rib and referenced to the right supraclavicular fossa according to the International 10-20 system. The ECG and EEG were recorded from both subjects simultaneously so that the data

---

58   Reidbord SP, Redington DJ. Nonlinear analysis of autonomic responses in a therapist during psychotherapy. *J Nerv Ment Dis* 1993; 181:428-435.

59   Marci CD. Psychophysiology and psychotherapy: The neurobiology of human relatedness. *Practical Reviews of Psychiatry* (Audio tape) 2002; 25(3).

60   McCraty R, Atkinson M, Tomasino D, Tiller W. The electricity of touch: Detection and measurement of cardiac energy exchange between people. In: Pribram K, ed. *Brain and Values: Is a Biological Science of Values Possible*. Mahwah, NJ: Lawrence Erlbaum Associates, 1998:359-379.

(typically sampled at 256 hertz or higher) could be analyzed for simultaneous signal detection in both.

To clarify the direction in which the signal flow was analyzed, the subject whose ECG R-wave was used as the time reference for the signal averaging procedure is referred to as the "signal source," or simply "source." The subject whose EEG was analyzed for the registration of the source's ECG signal is referred to as the "signal receiver," or simply "receiver." The number of averages used in the majority of the experiments was 250 ECG cycles (~ 4 minutes). The subjects did not consciously intend to send or receive a signal and, in most cases, were unaware of the true purpose of the experiments. The results of these experiments have led us to conclude that the nervous system acts as an antenna, which is tuned to and responds to the magnetic fields produced by the hearts of other individuals. My colleagues and I call this energetic information exchange cardioelectromagnetic communication and believe it to be an innate ability that heightens awareness and mediates important aspects of true empathy and sensitivity to others. Furthermore, we have observed that this energetic communication ability can be enhanced, resulting in a much deeper level of non-verbal communication, understanding, and connection between people. We also propose that this type of energetic communication between individuals may play a role in therapeutic interactions between clinicians and patients that has the potential to promote the healing process.

From an electrophysiological perspective, it appears that sensitivity to this form of energetic communication between individuals is related to the ability to be emotionally and physiologically coherent. The data indicate that when individuals are in the coherent mode, they are more sensitive to receiving information contained in the fields generated by others. In addition, during physiological coherence, internal systems are more stable, function more efficiently, and radiate electromagnetic fields containing a more coherent structure.[14]

The Electricity of Touch

The first step was to determine if the ECG signal of one person could be detected in another individual's EEG during physical contact. For these experiments we seated pairs of subjects 4 feet apart, during which time they were simultaneously monitored. An initial 10-minute baseline period (no physical contact) was followed by a 5-minute period in which subjects remained seated but reached out and held the hand of the other person (like shaking hands). Figure 5 shows a typical example of the results.

Prior to holding hands, there was no indication that Subject 1's ECG signals

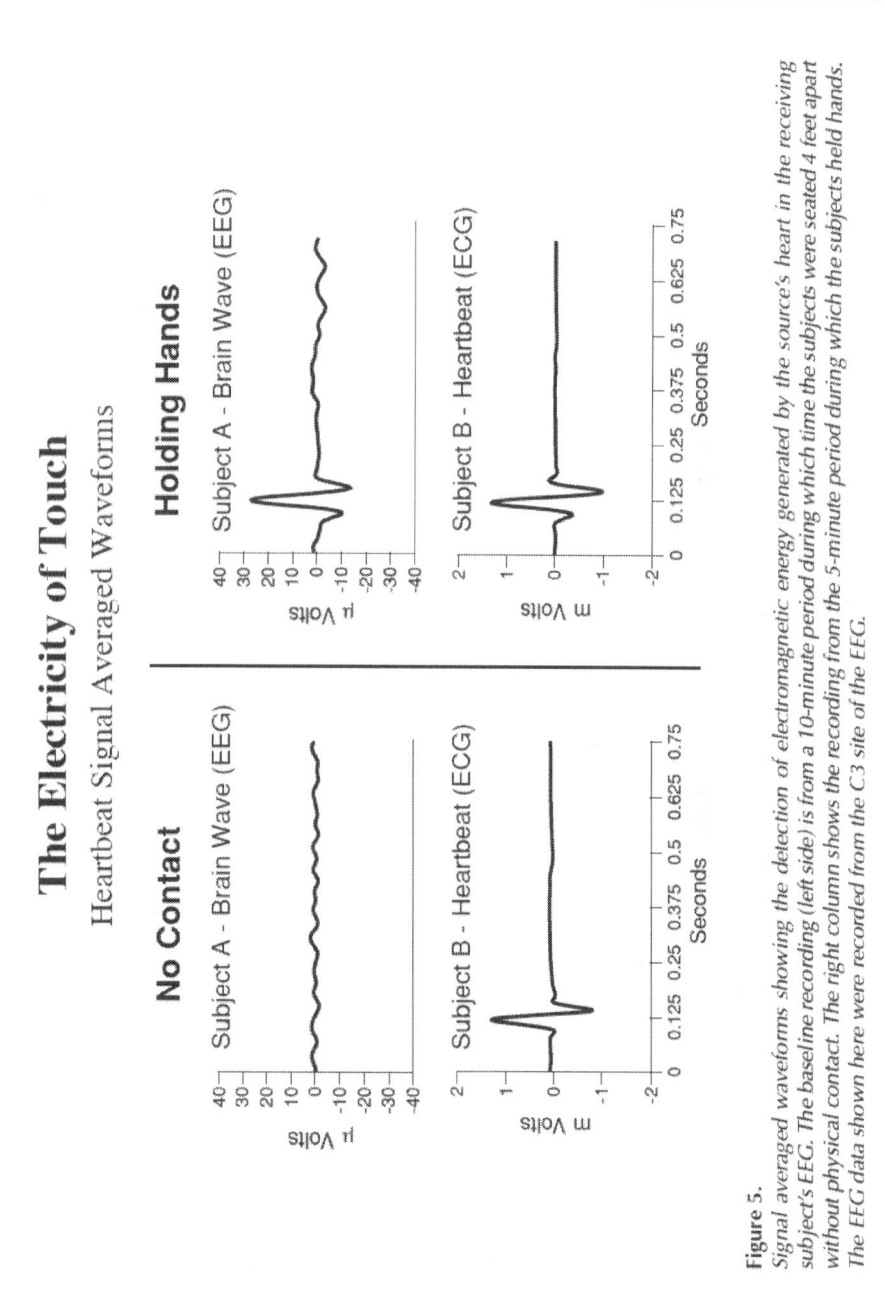

Figure 5.
Signal averaged waveforms showing the detection of electromagnetic energy generated by the source's heart in the receiving subject's EEG. The baseline recording (left side) is from a 10-minute period during which time the subjects were seated 4 feet apart without physical contact. The right column shows the recording from the 5-minute period during which the subjects held hands. The EEG data shown here were recorded from the C3 site of the EEG.

were detected in Subject 2's EEG. However, upon holding hands, Subject 1's ECG could be clearly detected in Subject 2's EEG at all monitored locations. While in most pairs a clear signal transfer between the two subjects was measurable in one direction, it was only observed in both directions simultaneously in about 30 percent of the pairs (i.e., Subject 2's ECG could be detected in Subject 1's EEG at the same time that Subject 1's ECG was detectable in Subject 2's EEG). From other experiments we have concluded that this phenomenon is not related to gender or amplitude of the ECG signal. As shown later, an important variable appears to be the degree of physiological coherence maintained.

After demonstrating that the ECG from one individual could be detected in another's EEG during physical contact, we completed a series of experiments to determine if the signal was transferred via electrical conduction through the skin alone or if it was also radiated. In one set of experiments subjects were recorded holding hands under two sets of conditions: barehanded and wearing form-fitting, latex lab gloves. The ECG signal of one subject could be clearly detected in the EEG of the other subject even when they were wearing the gloves; however, the signal amplitude was reduced approximately ten-fold. This suggests that while a significant degree of the signal transfer occurs through skin conduction, the signal is also radiated or capacitively coupled between individuals. When conductive gel was used to decrease skin-to-skin contact resistance, the signal amplitude was unaffected. For additional detail, the protocols and data from these and related experiments are described elsewhere.[61]

We also conducted several experiments to determine if the transfer of cardiac energy and information is affected by the orientation of the subjects' hand-holding (i.e., source's left hand holding receiver's right hand vs. source's right hand holding receiver's left hand, etc.). The subjects were instructed to hold hands in each of the four possible orientations for 5 minutes. Since we only performed this experiment with three subject pairs, the results should be interpreted with a degree of caution; how- ever, we did find that consistent and measurable differences could be observed. The source's ECG appeared with the largest amplitude in the receiver's EEG when the receiver's right hand was held by either the source's left or right hand. When the receiver's left hand was held by the source's right hand, the signal appeared at a lower amplitude. Finally, when the receiver's left hand was held by the source's left hand, the ECG signal was either very low in amplitude or undetectable.[60]

The possibility exists that in some cases the signal appearing in the receiving subject's recordings could be the receiver's own ECG rather than that of the other subject. Given the signal averaging procedure employed, this could

61   Russek L, Schwartz G. Interpersonal heart-brain registration and the perception of parental love: A 42 year follow- up of the Harvard Mastery of Stress Study. *Subtle Energies* 1994; 5:195-208.

only occur if the source's ECG was continually and precisely synchronized with the receiver's ECG. To definitively rule this out, the data in all experiments were checked for this possibility.

Simultaneously and independently, Russek and Schwartz at the University of Arizona conducted similar experiments in which they were also able to demonstrate the detection of an individual's cardiac signal in another's EEG recording in two people sitting quietly, without physical contact.[62] In a publication entitled *"Energy Cardiology,"* they discuss the implications of their findings in the context of what they call a "dynamical energy systems approach" describing the heart as a prime generator, organizer, and integrator of energy in the human body.[62]

Heart-Brain Synchronization During Non-physical Contact

Since the magnetic component of the field produced by the heartbeat is radiated outside the body and can be detected several feet away with SQUID-based magnetometers,[1] we further tested the transference of signals between subjects who were not in physical contact. In these experiments, the subjects were either seated side by side or facing each other at varying distances. In some cases, we were able to detect a clear QRS-shaped signal in the receiver's EEG, but not in others. Although the ability to obtain a clear registration of the ECG in the other person's EEG declined as the distance between subjects was increased, the phenomenon appears to be non-linear. For instance, a clear signal could be detected at a distance of 18 inches in one session but was undetectable in the very next trial at a distance of only 6 inches. Although transmission of a clear QRS-shaped signal is uncommon at distances over 6 inches in our experience, this does not preclude the possibility that physiologically relevant information can be communicated between people at longer distances.

Because of the apparent non-linear nature of the phenomenon and the growing body of data suggesting that the detection of weak periodic signals can be enhanced in biological systems via a mechanism known as stochastic resonance, we investigated the possibility that physiological coherence may be an important variable in determining whether the cardiac fields are detected past the 6-inch distance. The non-linear stochastic resonance model predicts that under certain circumstances, very weak coherent electromagnetic signals are detectable by biological systems and can have significant biological

---

62   Russek L, Schwartz G. Energy Cardiology: A dynamical energy systems approach for integrating conventional and alternative medicine. *Advances* 1996; 12:4-24.

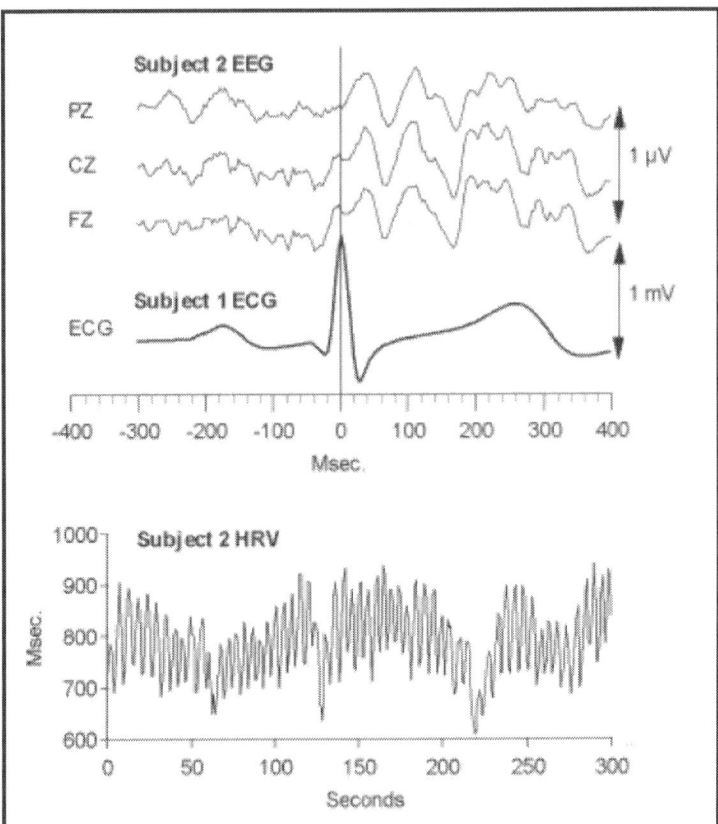

Figure 6. Heart-brain synchronization between two people.
The top three traces are Subject 2's signal averaged EEG waveforms, which are synchronized to the R-wave of Subject 1's ECG. The lower plot shows Subject 2's heart rate variability pattern, which was coherent throughout the majority of the record. The two subjects were seated at a conversational distance without physical contact.

effects.[63,64,65,66] Stochastic resonance will be discussed in more detail in a subsequent section.

Figure 6 shows the data from two subjects seated facing one another at a

63   Wiesenfeld K, Moss F. Stochastic resonance and the benefits of noise: From ice ages to crayfish and SQUIDs. *Nature* 1995; 373:33-36.

64   Bulsara AR, Gammaitoni L. Tuning into noise. *Physics Today* 1996; March:39-45.

65   Poponin V. Nonlinear stochastic resonance in weak EMF interactions with diamagnetic ions bound within proteins. In: Allen MJ, Cleary SF, Sower AE, eds. *Charge and Field Effects in Biosystems.* New Jersey: World Scientific, 1994:306-319.

66   Astumian RD, Weaver JC, Adair RK. Rectification and signal averaging of weak electric fields by biological cells. *Proc Natl Acad Sci USA* 1995; 92:740-743.

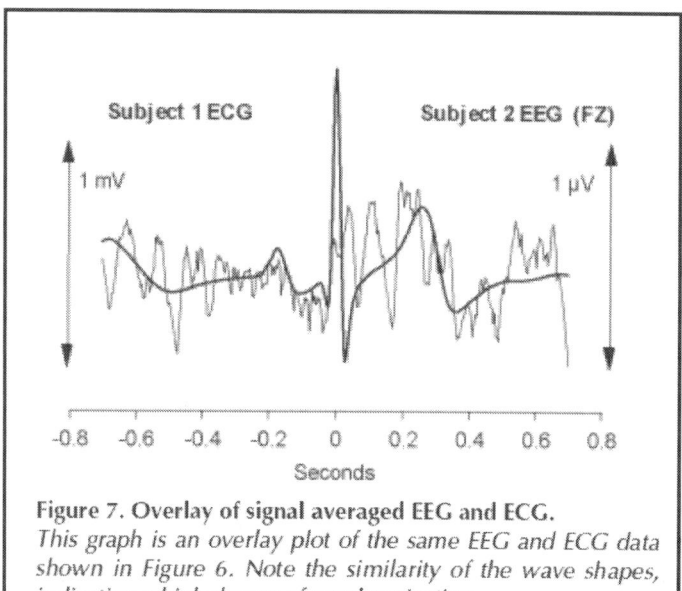

Figure 7. Overlay of signal averaged EEG and ECG.
This graph is an overlay plot of the same EEG and ECG data shown in Figure 6. Note the similarity of the wave shapes, indicating a high degree of synchronization.

distance of 5 feet, with no physical contact. The subjects were asked to use the Heart Lock-In technique,[39, 40] an emotional restructuring exercise that has been demonstrated to produce sustained states of physiological coherence when properly applied.[17] There was no intention to "send energy" and participants were not aware of the purpose of the experiment. The top three traces show the signal-averaged waveforms derived from the EEG locations along the medial line of the head.

Note that in this example, the signal averaged waveforms do not contain any semblance of the QRS complex shape as seen in the physical contact experiments; rather they reveal the occurrence of an alpha wave synchronization in the EEG of one subject that is precisely timed to the R-wave of the other subject's ECG. Power spectrum analysis of the signal averaged EEG waveforms was used to verify that it is the alpha rhythm that is synchronized to the other person's heart. This alpha synchronization does not imply that there is increased alpha activity, but it does show that the existing alpha rhythm is able to synchronize to extremely weak external electromagnetic fields such as those produced by another person's heart. It is well known that the alpha rhythm can synchronize to an external stimulus such as sound or light flashes, but the ability to synchronize to such a subtle electromagnetic signal is surprising. As mentioned, there is also a significant ratio of alpha activity that is synchronized to one's own heartbeat, and the amount of this synchronized alpha activity is significantly increased during periods of physiological coherence.[20, 21]

Figure 7 shows an overlay plot of one of Subject 2's signal averaged EEG trac-

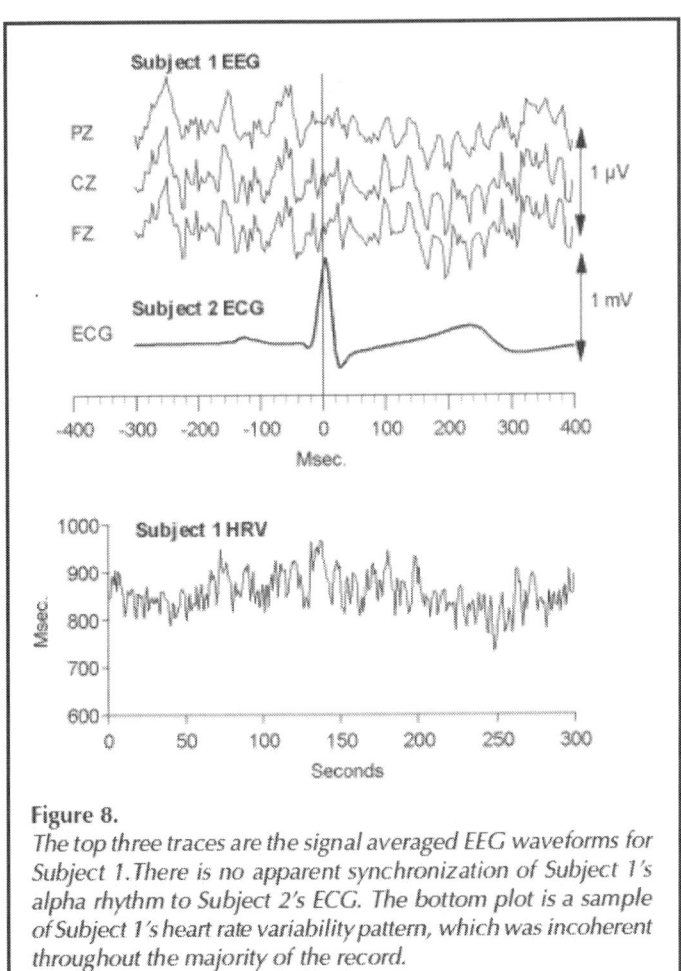

Figure 8.
The top three traces are the signal averaged EEG waveforms for Subject 1. There is no apparent synchronization of Subject 1's alpha rhythm to Subject 2's ECG. The bottom plot is a sample of Subject 1's heart rate variability pattern, which was incoherent throughout the majority of the record.

es and Subject 1's signal averaged ECG. This view shows an amazing degree of synchronization between the EEG of Subject 2 and Subject 1's heart. These data show that it is possible for the magnetic signals radiated by the heart of one individual to influence the brain rhythms of another. In addition, this phenomenon can occur at conversational distances. As yet, we have not tested this effect at distances greater than 5 feet.

Figure 8 shows the data from the same two subjects during the same time period, only it is analyzed for alpha synchronization in the opposite direction (Subject 1's EEG and Subject 2's ECG). In this case, we see that there is no observable synchronization between Subject 1's EEG and Subject 2's ECG. The key difference between the data shown in Figure 6 and Figure 8 is the high degree of physiological coherence maintained by Subject 2. In other words, the degree of coherence in the receiver's heart rhythms appears to determine whether his/

her brain waves synchronize to the other person's heart.

This suggests that when one is in a physiologically coherent mode, one exhibits greater sensitivity in registering the electromagnetic signals and information patterns encoded in the fields radiated by the hearts of other people. At first glance these data may be mistakenly interpreted as suggesting that we are more vulnerable to the potential negative influence of incoherent patterns radiated by those around us. In fact, the opposite is true, because when people are able to maintain the physiological coherence mode, they are more internally stable and thus less vulnerable to being negatively affected by the fields emanating from others. It appears that it is the increased internal stability and coherence that allows for the increased sensitivity to emerge.

This fits quite well with our experience in training thousands of individuals in how to self-generate and maintain coherence while they are listening to others during conversation. Once individuals learn this skill, it is a common experience that they become much more attuned to other people and are able to detect and understand the deeper meaning behind spoken words. They are often able to sense what someone else really wishes to communicate even when the other person may not be clear about that which he is attempting to say. This technique, called Intuitive Listening, helps people to feel fully heard and promotes greater rapport and empathy between people.[67]

Our data are also relevant to Russek and Schwartz's findings that people who are more accustomed to experiencing positive emotions such as love and care are better receivers of cardiac signals from others.[61] In their follow-up study of 20 college students, those who had rated themselves as having been raised by loving parents exhibited significantly greater registration of an experimenter's ECG in their EEG than others who had perceived their parents as less loving. Our findings, which show that positive emotions such as love, care, and appreciation are associated with increased physiological coherence, suggest the possibility that the subjects in Russek and Schwartz's study had higher ratios of physiological coherence, which could explain the greater registration of cardiac signals.

Heart Rhythm Entrainment Between Subjects

When heart rhythms are more coherent, the electromagnetic field that is radiated outside the body correspondingly becomes more organized, as shown in Figure 4. The data presented thus far indicate that signals and information can be communicated energetically between individuals, but so far have not implied a literal entrainment of two individuals' heart rhythm patterns. We have

---

67   Childre D, Cryer B. *From Chaos to Coherence: The Power to Change Performance.* Boulder Creek, CA: Planetary, 2000.

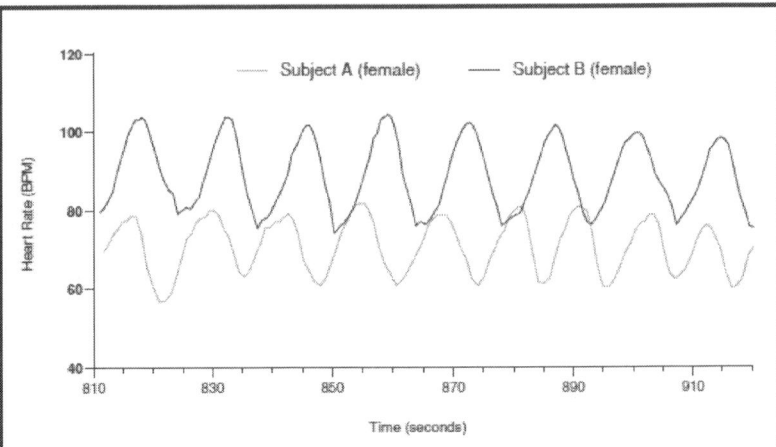

Figure 9. Heart rhythm entrainment between two people.
These data were recorded while both subjects were practicing the Heart Lock-In emotional restructuring technique and consciously feeling appreciation for each other. It should be emphasized that in typical waking states, entrainment between people such as in this example is rare.

found that entrainment of heart rhythm patterns between individuals is possible, but usually occurs only under very specific conditions. In our experience, true heart rhythm entrainment between individuals is very rare during normal waking states. We have found that individuals who have a close living or working relationship are the best candidates for exhibiting this type of entrainment. Figure 9 shows an example of heart rhythm entrainment between two women who have a close working relationship and practice coherence-building techniques regularly. For this experiment, they were seated 4 feet apart, and, although blind to the data, were consciously focused on generating feelings of appreciation for each other.

A more complex type of entrainment can also occur during sleep. Although we have only looked at couples who are in long-term stable and loving relationships, we have been surprised at the high degree of heart rhythm synchrony observed in these couples while they sleep. Figure 10 shows an example of a small segment of data from one couple. These data were recorded using an ambulatory ECG (Holter) recorder with a modified cable harness that allowed the concurrent recording of two individuals on the same tape. Note how the heart rhythms simultaneously change in the same direction and how heart rates converge. Throughout the recording, clear transition periods are evident in which

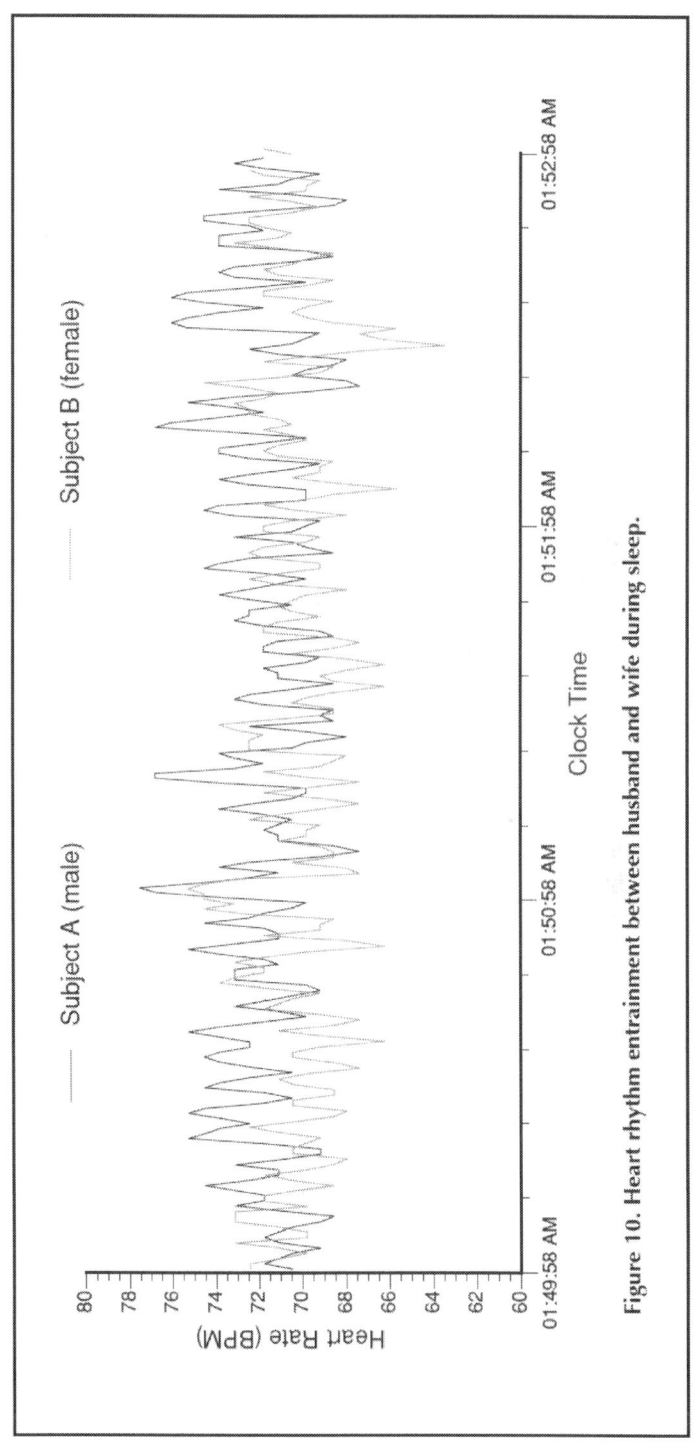

Figure 10. Heart rhythm entrainment between husband and wife during sleep.

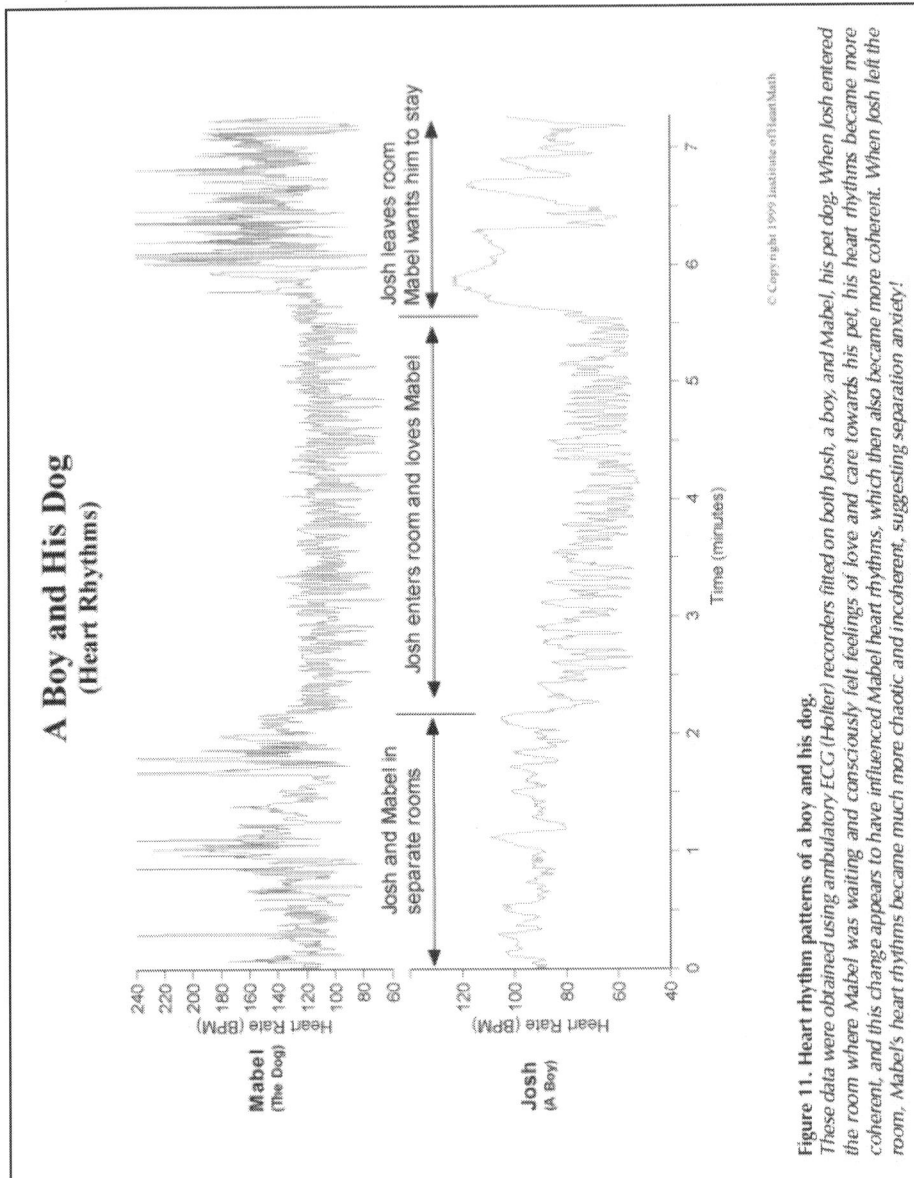

Figure 11. Heart rhythm patterns of a boy and his dog.
These data were obtained using ambulatory ECG (Holter) recorders fitted on both Josh, a boy, and Mabel, his pet dog. When Josh entered the room where Mabel was waiting and consciously felt feelings of love and care towards his pet, his heart rhythms became more coherent, and this change appears to have influenced Mabel heart rhythms, which then also became more coherent. When Josh left the room, Mabel's heart rhythms became much more chaotic and incoherent, suggesting separation anxiety!

the heart rhythms move into greater synchronicity, maintain the entrainment for some time, and then drift out again. This implies that unlike in most wakeful states, entrainment between the heart rhythms of individuals can and does occur during sleep.

We have also found that a type of heart rhythm entrainment or synchronization can occur in interactions between people and their pets. Figure 10 shows the results of an experiment looking at the heart rhythms of my son Josh (15 years old at the time of the recording) and his dog, Mabel. Here we used two Holter recorders, one fitted on Mabel and the other on Josh. We synchronized the recorders and placed Mabel in one of our labs. Josh then entered the room and sat down and proceeded to consciously feel feelings of love towards Mabel. Note the synchronous shift to increased coherence in the heart rhythms of both Josh and Mabel as Josh consciously feels love for his pet.

Influence of the Heart's Bioelectromagnetic Field on Cells

The idea that information can be communicated between biological systems and cause an effect in another living system is far from a new concept. This phenomenon has been examined in many different biological systems. A review of this literature is beyond the scope of this paper, but the subject has been reviewed recently by Marilyn Schlitz, Director of Research at the Institute of Noetic Sciences. In her review, both intention and how it is focused (i.e., attitude) are considered important variables in affecting outcomes.[68] Further, studies conducted in our laboratory suggest that emotional state and the degree of coherence in the electromagnetic fields produced by the heart are also important variables.

We have long suspected that one aspect of the heart's electromagnetic field acts as a carrier wave for information that can affect the function of cells in our own body as well as other biological systems in proximity. In the early 1990s, we undertook a series of experiments to test this hypothesis. This project evolved over several years and extended into many types of experiments. We were able to demonstrate that individuals can cause changes in the structure of water,[51] in cell growth rate, and in the conformational state of DNA.[52] In general, we found that in order to produce these effects in a reliable manner, both a high degree of heart rhythm coherence and an intention to produce a given change were critical.

Much scientific research has attempted to determine the effects, if any,

68   Schlitz M, Braud W. Distant intentionality and healing: Assessing the evidence. *Altern Ther Health Med* 1997; 3:62-73.

of electromagnetic fields (particularly the 50 and 60-hertz fields generated by power lines) on cells, and has yielded largely inconclusive results. However, comparatively little effort has been made to understand the effects of the body's endogenous fields, those that actually comprise the bioelectromagnetic environment in which our cells are continuously bathed. The most consistent and strongest source of an endogenous electromagnetic field is of course the heart.

In order to test the hypothesis that the electromagnetic field generated by the heart may have direct effects at the cellular level, we performed a series of cell culture experiments in which we exposed several different cell lines to simulated heart fields. To do this, we first acquired ECG data at a 10-kilohertz sample rate from people in various emotional states, generating correspondingly different heart rhythm patterns. We then used a digital-to-analog converter to recreate these ECG signals, which were fed into a specially built amplifier that could accurately recreate the low frequency portions of the ECG along with the higher frequencies. The output of the amplifier was used to drive a coil in which cell cultures were placed. For the experiment described here, a 2-inch diameter solenoid coil 15 inches high was placed vertically inside a 5% carbon dioxide incubator. Human fibroblasts (skin cells) were placed in 35-millimeter petri dishes inside the center section of the coils where the field was uniform. Typically, 10 individual petri dishes, each containing the same number of cells, were placed inside the coils. Identical cells were placed in a mock coil in a separate incubator and served as controls for each experiment. The field strength to which the cells in the human body are exposed from a normal heart-beat was determined. The output of the amplifier was adjusted so that the cells placed in the coil were exposed to approximately the same field strength as they would be in the body. While the cells were growing in the incubator over a 6-day period, they were continuously exposed to the ECG signals.

After exposure, the growth rates of the cells in the active and control coils were measured using a colorimetric staining assay. After many trials and variations of this basic experiment, we found that fibroblast cells exposed to the heart's field exhibited a mean increase in growth rate of 20% as compared to the controls. We also performed several trials in which we exposed the same type cells to a 60-hertz field of the same average magnitude of the heart's field. In this case, there was no significant change in the growth rate when compared to the controls. We did find a slight difference in the growth rate in cells exposed to coherent versus incoherent ECG signals. The coherent field yielded a higher growth rate; however, this effect did not reach statistical significance in this set of experiments. Thus, it appears that the presence or absence of a cardiac field was the primary variable to influence growth rate in these experiments.

One particularly intriguing experiment was performed in which healthy human fibroblasts and human fibrosarcoma cells (tumor cells from the same lineage) were both exposed to the same coherent ECG signal. We found that the growth of the healthy cells was facilitated by 20%, as expected, while the growth of the tumor cells was inhibited by 20%. These results may relate to work conducted in Germany by Ulrich Randoll with cancer patients. He has found that by monitoring a patient's own heartbeat and using it to trigger the application of an externally applied pulsed field, he has been able to successfully treat a number of patients with advanced carcinomas.[69] Dr. Randoll's therapeutic goal is to "regenerate and stabilize the basic autonomic rhythm of the organism." He has also used ultrastructural tomographic images of living cells to visualize temporal rhythms in the structural elements at the sub-cellular level. This technique shows clear differences in the temporal rhythms of cancer cells as compared to normal cells.[70] He is convinced that his treatments are helping to restore the normal pattern of activity at the cellular level, which facilitates recovery from disease, and believes that the rhythm of the heart and the field it produces are the key to this healing process.

Mechanisms of Weak Electromagnetic Field Effects in Biological Systems

A biological response to an external field (signal) implies that the signal has caused changes in the system greater than those caused by random fluctuating events, or noise. Theoretical estimates of the limitations on the detection of very small signals by sensory systems imposed by the presence of thermal noise (thermal noise limit) were traditionally made using linear approximation under the assumption that the system is in a state of equilibrium.[71] Traditional linear theory predicted that weak, extremely low frequency electromagnetic fields, such as that radiated from the human heart, could not generate enough energy to overcome the therma noise limit and thus affect biological systems. However, more recently it has been recognized that a linear and equilibrium approach is not appropriate for modeling biological systems, which are intrinsically nonlinear, nonequilibrium, and noisy. A number of experiments have revealed cellular responses to electromagnetic field magnitudes far smaller than the theoretical

---

69   Randoll U. The role of complex biophysical-chemical therapies for cancer. *Bioelectrochem Bioenerg* 1992; 27:341-346.

70   Randoll U, Dehmlow R, Regling G, Olbrich K. Ultrastructure tomographical observations of life processes as dependent on weak electromagnetic fields. *Dtch Zschr Onkol* 1994; 26:12-14.

71   Bialek W. Physical limits to sensation and perception. *Annu Rev Biophys Biophys Chem* 1987; 16:455-478.

estimates arrived at by linear modelling for the minimum field strength required to overcome the thermal noise limit in these systems.[72]

It has been proposed that this discrepancy can in part be accounted for by biological cells' capacity to rectify and essentially signal average weak oscillating electromagnetic fields through field-induced variation in the catalytic activity of membrane-associated enzymes or in the conformation of membrane channel proteins.[66,72] In addition to signal averaging by the cells, it has also been established that the noise in biological systems can play a constructive role in the detection of weak periodic signals via a mechanism known as stochastic resonance.[63-66] Stochasm is a Greek word that describes a system that is random but purposeful. In essence, stochastic resonance is a non-linear cooperative effect in which a weak, normally sub-threshold periodic (coherent) stimulus entrains ambient noise, resulting in the periodic signal becoming greatly enhanced and able to produce large-scale effects. The signature of stochastic resonance is noted by the signal-to-noise ratio in the system rising to a maximum at some optimal noise intensity, corresponding to the maximum cooperation between the signal and the noise. Essentially, the noise acts to boost a coherent, sub-threshold signal to a level above the threshold value, enabling it to generate measurable effects. Stochastic resonance is now known to occur in a wide range of biological systems and processes, including sensory transduction, neural signal processing, oscillating chemical reactions,[63,64] and intracellular calcium signalling.[73] In addition, coherent electromagnetic fields have been shown to produce substantially greater effects than incoherent signals on enzymatic pathways, such as the ornithine decarboxylase pathway.[74] Remarkably, experimental studies have documented effects of subthermal, coherent signals in different biological systems for signal amplitudes as small a one-tenth or even one-hundredth the amplitude of the random noise component.[75,76,77] As a weak signal becomes more coherent, the greater its capacity becomes to entrain ambient noise and thus produce significant effects.

72   Weaver JC, Astumian RD. The response of living cells to very weak electric fields: The thermal noise limit. *Science* 1990; 247:459-462.

73   Walleczek J. Field effects on cells of the immune system: The role of calcium signaling. *Fed Am Soc Exp Biol* 1992; 6:3177-3185.

74   Litovitz TA, Krause D, Mullins JM. Effect of coherence time of the applied magnetic field on ornithine decarboxylase activity. *Biochem Biophys Res Commun* 1991; 178:862-865.

75   Bezrukov SM, Vodyanoy I. Noise-induced enhancement of signal transduction across voltage-dependent ion channels. *Nature* 1995; 378:362-364.

76   Levin JE, Miller JP. Broadband neural encoding in the cricket cercal sensory system enhanced by stochastic resonance. *Nature* 1996; 380:165-168.

77   Bezrukov SM, Vodyanoy I. Stochastic resonance in nondynamical systems without response thresholds. *Nature* 1997; 385:319-321.

Thus, cellular signal averaging and non-linear stochastic resonance provide potential mechanisms by which increased heart rhythm coherence may produce significant biological effects, both within and between people. For example, through such mechanisms, the consistent self-induction of sustained states of physiological coherence by an individual may give rise to changes at the cellular level that may enhance health and healing. Alternatively, a clinician's coherent cardiac field, which is detected by a patient, may be amplified in such a way as to positively affect the patient's physiology. The importance of signal coherence in this model also suggests that further attention be given to the contribution of heartfelt positive emotions and attitudes, as drivers of coherence, in the healing process. It is possible that the generation of physiological coherence and biological effects produced by this beneficial mode may in part explain the observed relationship between positive emotions and favorable health outcomes, as well as the emphasis that many therapeutic practices place on the development of a mutually caring relationship between practitioner and patient.[60] Furthermore, it is likely that the therapeutic value of interventions that facilitate the generation and maintenance of sustained feelings of appreciation, care, and love may derive in part from bioelectromagnetically-mediated effects on cellular physiology.

Conclusions and Implications for Clinical Practice

Bioelectromagnetic communication is a real phenomenon that has numerous implications for physical, mental, and emotional health. This paper has focused on the proposition that increasing the coherence within and between the body's endogenous bioelectromagnetic systems can increase physiological and metabolic energy efficiency, promote mental and emotional stability, and provide a variety of health rewards. It is further proposed that many of the benefits of increased physiological coherence will ultimately prove to be mediated by processes and interactions occurring at the electromagnetic or energetic level of the organism.

With the many physiological and psychological benefits that increased coherence appears to offer, helping patients learn to self-generate and sustain this psychophysiological mode with increased consistency in their day-to-day lives provides a new strategy for clinicians to assist their patients on multiple levels. There are several straightforward ways to help patients increase their physiological coherence. Teaching and guiding them in the practice of positive emotion refocusing and emotional restructuring techniques in conjunction with heart rhythm feedback has proved to be a simple and cost-effective approach to improving patient outcomes. These coherence-building methods are not only ef-

47

fective therapeutic tools in and of themselves, but by increasing synchronization and harmony among the body's internal systems, may also help increase a patient's physiological receptivity to the therapeutic effects of other treatments.

Coherence-building approaches may also help health care practitioners increase their effectiveness in working with patients. In self-generating a state of physiological coherence, the clinician has the potential to facilitate the healing process by establishing a coherent pattern in the subtle electromagnetic environment to which patients are exposed. Since even very weak coherent signals have been found to give rise to significant effects in biological systems, it is possible that such coherent heart fields may provide unexpected therapeutic benefits. Furthermore, by increasing coherence, clinicians may not only enhance their own mental acuity and emotional stability, but may also develop increased sensitivity to subtle electromagnetic information in their environment. This, in turn, could potentially enable a deeper intuitive connection and communication between practitioner and patient, which can be a crucial component of the healing process.

In conclusion, I believe that the electromagnetic energy generated by the heart is an untapped resource within the human system awaiting further exploration and application. Acting as a synchronizing force within the body, a key carrier of emotional information, and an apparent mediator of a type of subtle electromagnetic communication between people, the cardiac bioelectromagnetic field may have much to teach us about the inner dynamics of health and disease as well as our interactions with others.

Rollin McCraty, Ph.D. is Director of Research of the HeartMath Research Center at the Institute of HeartMath. He is also an Adjunct Professor at Clemson University and Visiting Professor in the Department of Family and Community Medicine at the University of Alabama at Birmingham. A psychophysiologist, Dr. McCraty's research interests include the physiology of optimal function with a focus on the mechanisms by which emotions influence cognitive processes, behavior, and health as well as the global interconnectivity between people and the earth's energetic systems. Findings from this research have been applied to the development of tools and technology to optimize individual and organizational health, performance, and quality of life. He is a Fellow of the American Institute of Stress, holds memberships with the International Neurocardiology Network, American Autonomic Society, Pavlovian Society and Association for Applied Psychophysiology and Biofeedback among others. Dr. McCraty has acted as Principal Investigator in numerous laboratory research studies examining the effects of emotions on heart–brain interactions and on autonomic, cardiovascular, hormonal, and immune system function. He has also served as PI in a number of field studies to determine the outcomes of positive emotion-focused interventions and heart rhythm feedback in diverse organizational and educational settings as well as in various clinical populations. His research has been published in journals that include the American Journal of Cardiology, Journal of the American College of Cardiology, Stress Medicine, Biological Psychology and Integrative Physiological and Behavioral Science.

HIDDEN THERAPEUTIC DIALOGUE:
DECODING THE LANGUAGE OF THE HUMAN HEART

JAMES J. LYNCH

We are, in a certain sense, living in an era comparable to Middleburg, Holland at the dawn of the 17th century. Though difficult to conceive, it was in this tiny Dutch town that two technological developments suddenly appeared that inexorably changed how mankind would come to view both their external and internal worlds. The first was the development of lenses that could be paired together to create the first binoculars, called "Lippershey's Looker". First crafted by Hans Lippershey in the early 1600s, his attempt to sell this device to the Italian Army led the Italian Senate to forward the device to Galileo for his scientific evaluation. Immediately recognizing the importance of this technological breakthrough, Galileo quickly increased the power of "Lippershey's Looker", and within a few months had crafted the first telescope. In 1610, Galileo published a small pamphlet entitled "Starry Messenger", in which he reported that his telescope allowed him to see at least ten times as many stars as were visible with the naked eye, that the moon contained a series of high mountains and was not a flat surface, and most importantly, he observed over the course of a few nights that there were four moons orbiting around Jupiter. He immediately deduced that Copernicus was correct, and that Aristotle's cosmology was wrong. The earth was not the center of the universe, but was itself orbiting around the sun. Then within a few decades, Hans Jansen and Antonie van Leeuwenhoek crafted the first of a series of microscopes that allowed scientists to peer ever deeper into the internal universe, and see for the first time, among many other crucial biological functions, the action of the capillary system.

Though it is often asserted that Galileo's discoveries led him to clash with the Catholic Church, the real struggle was his challenge to Aristotelian cosmology, which up to that time had dominated thinking in Western European universities. Indeed Copernicus' heliocentric views were warmly greeted by the Roman Curia 100 years earlier, and he had been invited to present his ideas to the Pope shortly before his death. What occurred in the century between Copernicus and Galileo, however, was Martin Luther's challenge to Papal authority, which had the unfortunate consequence of hardening philosophical attitudes toward the dangers posed by new ideas. In a hierarchical sense, Aristotle's philosophy dominated all Catholic universities in Europe, and his writings were viewed as a comprehensive and systematic framework that gave meaning to all of the other sciences in the university system. His cosmology was largely inherited from

49

Ptolemy, and represented but a tiny fraction of his much more important views on epistemology, politics, and the nature of the hierarchy of souls in living matter. Also embedded in Aristotle's philosophy were the links between the human heart, the human soul and our unique capacity to talk. Aristotle's hierarchy of souls was postulated to be the source of vitality for all living matter. Even more important were his discussions of man as far more than a social animal, but a political animal as well. "Political" was derived from the Greek word *polis*, which asserted that man was but one among many men. With the sudden appearance of scientific discoveries that challenged various aspects of his theory, unfortunately what subsequently occurred was the unexamined tossing out of the Aristotelian baby with the tainted bath water of his cosmology.

And into this philosophical vacuum in the early 17th century rushed an entirely new philosophy, one enunciated by René Descartes, and summarized in his famous dictum: *cogito ergo sum* – "I think, therefore I am." The allure of Cartesian thinking was that it offered a way to extract the Catholic Church from the "body business", thus avoiding the errors of Aristotle's cosmology and returning the Catholic Church to its proper concern for the human soul. In what was a grand restatement of the ancient biblical mandate to "render . . . unto Caesar the things which are Caesar's; and unto God the things that are God's" (Matthew 22:21), the new Cartesian dictum was to render unto the new Caesar—science—all bodies in the universe (whether they be solar or cellular, human or animal) and unto God the slim pickings that were left behind—the human soul. The original assumption that science was part of "Scientia", that is, wisdom, was replaced by the notion of science with a small "s", a method to understand physical reality.

Descartes' new philosophy and new scientific perspectives emerged just as certain of the assumptions of Aristotle's cosmology were challenged by a variety of new scientific observations, and it was sweeping in its overall conceptions: all bodies in nature, including the human body, operated as mechanical clockwork. But unlike all other bodies in the universe, human beings possessed a soul, which interacted with the machine body at the locus of the pineal gland. Those phenomena that were traditionally considered to be uniquely human, including consciousness and cognition, and most importantly our capacity to speak, were assumed by Descartes to be attributes of the human soul. The souls of plants and animals were dispensed with without discussion; Descartes simply asserted that they were just lower forms of machines. Gone, too, was the Aristotelian idea of the essential capacity of human beings to relate to plants and animals, as well as to other human beings, because human beings possessed all the attributes of plant and animal souls, as well as unique aspects of the human soul.

But it was his *cogito ergo sum* that left Descartes with the certainty that he existed because he could think about it. Descartes could never have asserted "I feel therefore I am" without first admitting that he had reduced feelings to imprecise thoughts that were decoded by the human soul at the locus of the pineal gland. Between 1605 and 1865, Descartes' concept of the human soul gradually evolved, and eventually was replaced by a new scientific term, the "mind", which proved to be the conceptual foundation of the dualistic concepts that still permeate modern psychology, the so-called mind/body interactions.

In his book *On the Origin of the Species*, Darwin extended Descartes' ideas one step further when he asserted that human bodies were qualitatively similar to animal bodies (the central core of Cartesian philosophy), and then subsequently added that the expression of emotions in men and animals were also qualitatively the same. Emotions, the so-called "e-motere" which were the biochemical perturbations that moved machine bodies in space, were a fundamental principal of Cartesian thinking. Unlike other animals which did possess a soul, it was only human beings possessing souls who could decode these *emotere* and thus through the power of the soul recognize them as imprecise thoughts. This was the essential difference between human machine bodies and animal machine bodies. Both moved in space by the power of biochemical perturbations, but only human beings could decode these emotere and thus come to know or recognize them. The foundations had been laid that would eventually lead to the removal of the concept of a soul from the human body (since human bodies were now similar to animal bodies), and replace it with a new word: "the mind/brain". The grand bargain had been completed, and the slim pickings of a "soul" that had been originally left to God now removed and brought under the province of the new Caesar, science. Psychology, and its literal meaning as the study of the soul, was now recast as the scientific study of human behavior and the study of reflexology. In rapid order, Pavlov and Freud appeared on the scene to lay the foundations for an entirely new 20th century science of psychology and psychiatry, and eventually even the concept of "neuropsychiatry".

Lost in this philosophical revolution was the importance of Descartes' belief that the human heart was nothing more and nothing less than a "heater" pump. Lost, as well, was the Aristotelian concept of the human heart as the center of all human relatedness. Aristotle's central assumption was that human beings were one among many, thus far more than social animals and essentially political as well, because they could talk and share the passions of their souls in dialogue. Also lost was the meaning of Blaise Pascal's challenge to Descartes in his *Pensees*, when he asserted: "The heart has its reasons, which the reason knows not . . . Do you love by reason?" Pascal instantly recognized that René Descartes had removed language from the human heart, made it an exclusive attribute of the soul, and completely confused the difference between emotions and feelings. In the Cartesian new world order, it was not mechanical hearts that could relate, but only human souls. Bodies, whether they were animal or human, could only interact in a stimulus–response manner, and certainly were not the source of human relatedness. The potential of the human heart to love, the potential of human bodies to relate to either other human bodies or animal bodies had been, so to speak, purged from human consciousness, almost as if some grand master had hit the "Alt-Delete" button in a computer. (The historical implications for modern views of the nature of the human cardiovascular system are outlined elsewhere in this issue by Paul Rosch.)

Late in the 20th century, a new technology emerged that was destined to have an impact every bit as significant as the 17th-century invention of the telescope and microscope that led to the overthrow of Aristotle's cosmology. Curiously this new technology allowed one to simultaneously peer inward, into the cardiovascular system of the human body as well as outward into the larger universe, to watch the way this hidden internal universe was in constant dialogue with the external universe. More importantly, this technology gradually forced a re-examination of the overarching Cartesian philosophical assumptions that had guided virtually all psychological research (including our own research) throughout the 20th century. Ever so slowly, this new computerized blood pressure technology led us to revisit the Aristotelian baby that had been tossed out with the dirty bath water of his cosmology 400 years earlier. What gradually emerged was a new way to more fully appreciate the dialogical nature of the human cardiovascular system, and a new appreciation for the fact that the entire human body was inextricably involved in a constant dialogue with the external universe. Gradually we began to recognize that this hidden bodily dialogue had to be understood and decoded in order to engage in a more meaningful psychotherapeutic dialogue.

When the new automated blood pressure monitoring device first appeared, however, we uncritically assumed that it was merely a new technological advance, a new way to measure blood pressure on a minute-to-minute basis. The old method involved the use of a stethoscope and mercury manometer, along with a manually inflated cuff. What was initially overlooked was that the old methods used to measure blood pressure required silence in order to hear the Korotkoff sounds, while the new computerized method permitted a person to continue talking while his or her blood pressure was measured through a process of oscillometry.

Initially, we watched with a mixture of incredulity and amazement at the remarkable ways that human blood pressure could be altered during dialogue, while scarcely considering the philosophical implications of what we were observing. We began to recognize that if we peered into Galileo's telescope, our blood pressure would fall way below its resting levels; and while his Starry Nights revealed the four Medician "stars" orbiting around Jupiter, Galileo had not yet conceived that René Descartes was wrong when he asserted that the human heart was a mere heater pump, that we did not love by reason, and that our hearts were inextricably joined in dialogue to a universe that was far more than mere mechanical clockwork.

It took almost a decade of scientific research to recognize that there was a "Language of the Human Heart", and that our bodies were in constant conversation with the universe beyond the confines of our individual and separate human bodies. We were, in fact, in constant heartfelt communication with the universe. [1]

Philosophy functions very much like air; it is seldom examined until it gets so polluted that we can no longer breathe. That was certainly true when I began my own graduate research at the Pavlovian Laboratories at the Johns Hopkins University Medical School and the Pavlovian Laboratories at the Perry Point VA hospital in Maryland in 1962. The Director of these laboratories was W. Horsley Gantt, M.D., a psychiatrist who had studied for seven years with Ivan P. Pavlov from 1922 to 1929 in St. Petersburg, Russia. When he returned to the Johns Hopkins Medical School in 1929, Dr. Gantt opened the first Pavlovian Laboratory in the United States. He helped to introduce Pavlov's research and writings into the English-speaking world. He translated Pavlov's lectures and research findings into English and began to faithfully apply his scientific methods to the study of the cardiovascular system [2]. If ever there was a University center that embraced the philosophy of René Descartes, it certainly was deeply rooted in the perspective guiding the research studies conducted in these laboratories. Pavlov himself had asserted on numerous occasions that René Descartes and Charles Darwin were the two major influences determining all of his own research studies. For example, at the beginning of his book *Conditioned Reflexes* (translated by G.V. Anrep) Pavlov noted:

"The physiologist must thus take his own path, when a trail has already been blazed for him. Three hundred years ago, Descartes evolved the idea of the reflex. Starting from the assumption that animals behaved simply as machines, he regarded every activity of the organism as a necessary reaction to some external stimulus…Descartes' conception of the reflex was constantly and fruitfully applied in these studies…" (Lecture 1)

Although the philosophy of René Descartes permeated the research atmosphere in these laboratories, I was unaware of Pavlov's mechanistic assumptions when I first met Dr. Gantt in 1962. What caught my attention was the intellectual excitement and challenges that pervaded the atmosphere of those laboratories. It was a privilege to have accidentally met a remarkable teacher in a fascinating research environment.

Three streams of research were particularly intriguing:

1) The first was the concept that there was an internal cardiovascular universe that could be conditioned in the exact same way that salivation could be conditioned. Well aware of the traditional Pavlovian model of a dog salivating to a tone that had been paired repeatedly with meat, a variant of this model was used to study the cardiovascular system of dogs. Typically a tone was paired with a mild electrical shock to the forepaw of the dog. After one or two pairings of the tone with shock, there was an immediate increase in heart rate and blood pressure whenever the tone was sounded. This was called the cardiovascular conditional reflex. By contrast it took 10-20 trials of the pairing of the tone with shock for the dog to begin lifting his paw during the same tone…the somatic component of the conditional reflex. Thus, there was a split, or what Dr. Gantt called a schizokinesis, between the somatic skeletal learning and the rapid conditioning of the autonomic nervous system. Even more intriguing was the process of extinction. If the tone was no longer paired with electric shock, then after ten to fifteen trials the dog would no longer lift his paw. The skeletal conditional reflexes could be rapidly extinguished. Yet the autonomic reactions, the blood pressure, and heart rate reactions were far more resistant to extinction and often would get more exaggerated over time. It was as if the heart hard a very difficult time forgetting, and in some instances, simply could not forget. [3]

A PAVLOVIAN CHAMBER

2) The second stream of research, and one that would come to dominate my own research interest, was a phenomenon that Dr. Gantt had labeled the "Effect of Person". The very nature of Pavlovian research required that the dog be placed in an environmentally controlled chamber and kept isolated from all external stimuli.

Since the cardiovascular system of the dog was being continuously monitored, it was soon apparent that whenever a human being merely entered the chamber, there would be a rapid increase in blood pressure and heart rate. Paradoxically, if the person then petted the dog, heart rate and blood pressure would quickly fall below baseline levels, sometimes falling over 50% below baseline measures. The dramatic nature of these cardiovascular responses to human touch was astonishing, and they left a lasting impression that would come to permeate most of my own subsequent research studies. [4]

In my own very first experiment on this "Effect of Person", it was observed that petting a dog could completely abolish both the conditional and the unconditional cardiovascular reflexes to electric shock. See the picture of the remarkable reactions to human petting in dogs. Human touch, it seemed, could abolish both the conditional reactions, as well as the unconditionally reflexive reactions, to painful electric shock. [5]

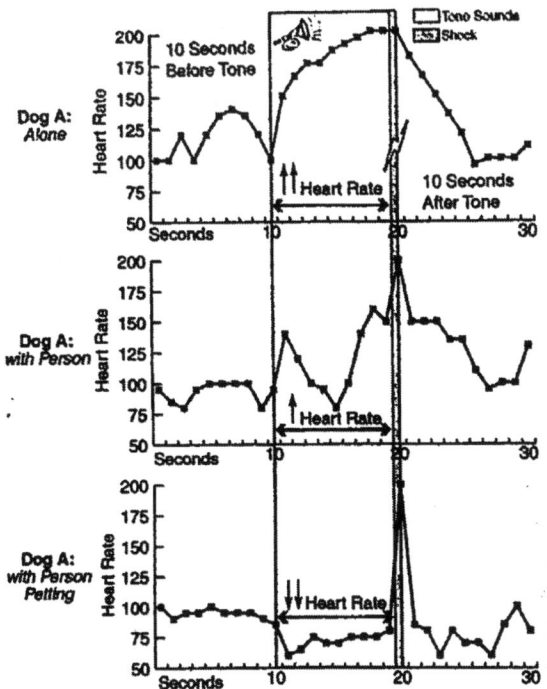

3) The third stream of research involved an analysis of the cardiovascular components of what Pavlov had called the orienting reflex. This phenomenon, routinely observed in dogs as well as human beings, would eventually emerge as a core concept involved in the hidden dialogue of psychotherapy. Basically, all higher animals, including human beings, exhibit significant drops in heart rate and blood pressure, as well as blood flow when they attend or "orient" to stimuli in the external environment. In dogs, for example, if

GRAPH OF HUMAN PETTING ABOLISHING CARDIAC CONDITIONAL AND UNCONDITIONAL RESPONSES TO PAIN

you sound a soft tone, you will readily observe that the dog will cock its ears, and orient towards the source of this external stimulation. Just as soon as it begins to "orient", or take in the external world, an abrupt and significant fall in heart rate and blood pressure occurs. [6]

A decade later, we would come to more fully appreciate that attempts to get patients to pay attention to the external world, to essentially "look out outside the confines of their own skin", could have immediate and powerful therapeutic benefits on the human cardiovascular system. It would prove to be a powerful therapeutic tool in helping patients to "reorient", to look outside, and to pay attention to a world beyond the confines of themselves.

These three notions,
1) the rapid conditioning of autonomic cardiovascular reflexes, and their resistance to rapid extinction,
2) the Effect of Person, and
3) the cardiovascular components of the orienting reflex would eventually form the foundations of an entirely new way to assist patients struggling with a wide variety of stressful issues in psychotherapy.

Examining the Effect of Person in Coronary Care and Shock Trauma Units

Around 1970, our attention began to shift away from animal research to human beings. The transition was stimulated by a basic question: if the cardiovascular system of animals responded in highly significant ways to human touch, would human beings also react in a similar manner? Could human touch literally touch the human heart?

Critical care units in hospitals monitor the heart rate and sometimes the blood pressure of patients on a continual basis, thus, they provide a natural ethological setting to study questions such as the effects of pulse palpation, or the

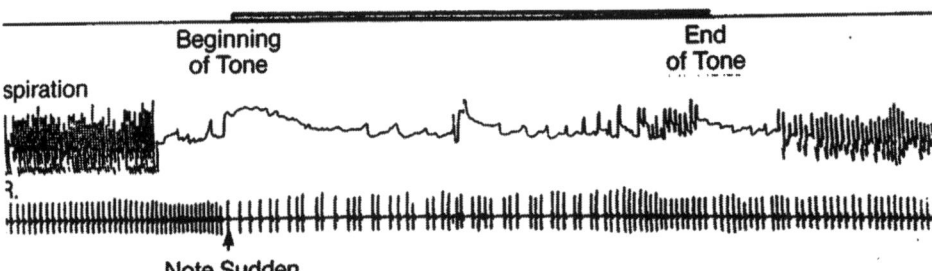

ABRUPT FALL IN HEART RATE IN A DOG LISTENING OR
ORIENTING TO A SOFT SOUND

visits from mates and friends on cardiac patients without doing any invasive research. Evidence rapidly began to accumulate that even the simple touch of a nurse palpating a coronary care patient's pulse could elicit highly significant changes in heart rate and heart rhythm. Indeed, in patients exhibiting a high frequency of ventricular arrhythmias, there was an immediate and highly significant reduction in the frequency of these arrhythmias to pulse palpation. Visits by family members could also evoke highly significant changes in heart rate and rhythm. [7]

In spite of the ubiquity of these reactions to human contact, it was far more difficult to isolate the specific cause of these cardiac reactions. Was it due specifically to touch, for example, or did human touch lead to changes in breathing patterns and muscle movements which then affected the heart?

Subsequent studies of patients in a University Shock Trauma unit provided dramatic evidence that touch itself had a powerful effect on the human heart. The patients in the Shock Trauma Unit of the University of Maryland were quite different than patients in a coronary care unit. They were victims of car accidents, for example, and usually did not have heart disease, were almost always given d-tubocurarine to control spasmodic muscle movements and their breathing was controlled by a respirator. Typically, they were also in comas and much younger than patients in coronary care. Yet the simple touch of a nurse, or simply the patient's hand being held, could elicit significant reductions in heart rate, as well as alterations in heart rhythm in these patients. [8]

Even heart transplant patients with totally denervated hearts exhibited powerful changes in blood pressure and heart rate to human communications, as well as to human touch. There was an immediate rise in blood pressure when they spoke, even though they were on high dosages of medication to control their blood pressure. Treatment of these patients showed that within ten sessions, there was a significant reduction in their blood pressure as well as their heart rate, suggesting that neurohumoral factors helped to lower their heart rate. [9]

Over a period of four to five years, the results of these studies began to elicit interest in an alternative question: if transient human touch and transient human contact could have powerful effects on the heart rate and the heart rhythm of patients in intensive care units, what were the consequences of the chronic absence of human contact? What were the medical consequences of human loneliness? In what turned out to be a fortuitous coincidence, the 1960 health census was the very first to consider whether marital status might be an important statistical variable in health and illness. Prior to that, marital status had not been considered vital to health. It took epidemiologists almost a decade to analyze the census data, and when the results finally became available, we were just completing the first series of studies in the coronary care and shock trauma units.

The health statistics were startling in their consistency. Single, widowed and divorced people in the United States were dying at rates 2–10 times higher than married people!

The Broken Heart: The Medical Consequences of Loneliness was published in 1977 [10] and was the first to document that the concept of a "broken heart" was far more than a poetic image for loneliness and despair, it was an overwhelming medical reality. In a society that seemed to be growing ever more fragmented, the lack of human companionship, chronic loneliness and social isolation, as well as the sudden loss of loved ones ranked among the leading causes of premature death in America. And while the lack of companionship was related to virtually every major disease, from cancer and tuberculosis to mental illness, the impact seemed to be particularly marked in the case of heart disease. At every age, all races, and both sexes, those who lived alone were at a significantly higher risk to die prematurely.

While we assumed that loneliness was the underlying lethal force that was contributing to these marked increases in premature disease and death, it was also apparent that not every divorced, single and widowed individual was lonely, nor were all married people living in states of marital bliss. Ironically this statistical "noise" and "variance in the health statistics" made it seem likely that the underlying hypothesis of the lethal impact of chronic loneliness deserved

far more scrutiny. If the central lethal force was loneliness, then efforts aimed at isolating this core toxic threat would undoubtedly greatly amplify the differences in mortality that the census data revealed.

Even more importantly were the issues involving the physiological mechanisms. Though the mortality statistics literally leaped out of the pages of the census data, it was far from clear how human loneliness could lead to a doubling of the incidence of coronary heart disease or a quadrupling of the incidence of hypertension. How in the world did loneliness, for example, contribute to a hardening of one's arteries?

Yet the greatest challenge was posed almost immediately by a cardiologist in charge of the University of Maryland Coronary Care Unit who challenged us with a certain degree of impatience: "If human loneliness is as lethal as the data seemed to indicate, then do something about it! Why not try to help hypertensive patients who are lonely to lower their blood pressure?"

Even before we could address any of these mechanistic questions, a distinguished University professor who appeared to fit all of the risk criteria that had been discussed in *The Broken Heart* sought our help to control his blood pressure. He was single, in his mid-fifties, mildly overweight, had already suffered a myocardial infraction, and was exhibiting symptoms of transient ischemia with labile hypertension.

Without a specific plan or course of action, we had arrived at an unanticipated crossroad, and the existing research data was not very encouraging. While it seemed intuitively obvious that psychotherapy would be the best way to deal with issues of human loneliness and human relatedness, the existing research data were replete with warnings. The overall conclusion was that psychotherapy was contraindicated for patients suffering from various forms of heart disease. It seemed to put them at greater risk!

Traditional Psychotherapy and Heart Disease

The mid-1970's was a period that was awash in a number of new non-pharmacological approaches to the treatment of hypertension. There were two, in particular, including the newly emergent field of biofeedback which offered the hope of using operant conditioning to control blood pressure, as well as the *The Relaxation Response* popularized by Herbert Benson, M.D. at Harvard University Medical School.

While the biofeedback approach first appeared to offer a significant new treatment modality, it was subsequently shown to produce little in the way of a clinical efficacy. We were well aware of the original promises that biofeedback could be used to help control the autonomic nervous system were fraught with empirical and epistemological pitfalls. [11]

The relaxation response initially appeared to be slightly more helpful. Yet while the reductions in blood pressure produced by these techniques were "statistically significant", the few millimeters of pressure reduction were not clinically robust. [12]

Earlier attempts to use non-pharmacological methods to help control hypertension were even more unsettling. In 1939, for example, Franz Alexander reported on the first of what would be a large number of studies attempting to use insight-oriented psychotherapy to help hypertensive patients to lower their blood pressure. These studies were initiated when there was no effective pharmacological agent that could help lower blood pressure. Sympathectomy, with all of the attendant adverse consequences, appeared to be the only way to help hypertensive patients avoid the catastrophic consequences of extreme hypertension. [13]

Based on the pioneering research of Walter Cannon, it was generally understood that hypertension was one component of chronic fight/flight reactions to stress, and with no effective medication, some way to manage this life-threatening problem was urgently needed. Alexander hypothesized that deeply hidden emotional conflicts were the principle cause of hypertension, and he assumed that psychoanalytically-oriented psychotherapy would be the best way to uncover the conflicts, and thus help patients to lower their blood pressure.

Alexander based his hypothesis on the psychoanalytic studies of Sigmund Freud, as well as the classic physiological studies of Walter Cannon. He hoped to bridge the gap between these two investigators. Cannon's book *Bodily Changes in Pain, Hunger, Fear and Rage* (1929) described the autonomic and neuroendocrine systems influences on the cardiovascular system. His book was the first to emphasize the crucial role that emotional stress played in the development of this disease. Although it had long been recognized that stress plays a vital role in the development of heart disease, Cannon's pioneering studies were the first to delineate the physiological mechanisms. He began to describe what he called the fight/flight response. He reasoned that in times of stress or emotional upheaval, the body had to have the adaptive capacity to either fight for survival or to flee.

Deeply influenced by this scientific perspective, Alexander assumed that hypertension was, in all likelihood, the end result of unconscious conflicts that placed a person in a state of hypervigilance, or a chronic state of unconscious fight/flight. For two decades, Alexander studied the personality of hypertensive individuals in order to better understand the nature of their conflicts, as well as to evaluate whether psychotherapy could be used to help alleviate their struggles, and thus lower their blood pressure.

While these studies are described in great detail elsewhere in *The Language of the Heart* [14], basically Alexander found that there was a systematic pattern of conflicts that could be traced back to childhood. In most cases, the conflicts had to do with dysfunctional parent-child communications. The infantile needs to be taken care of and to be understood were not adequately met and thus the person grew up driven to seek support and affection. This led the person to form dependent relationships, thus becoming trapped in a vicious circle, especially in regards to the open expression of anger. The patient thus found themselves torn apart by a chronic struggle against overtly expressing hostile impulses, and always trying to appear outwardly friendly in order to be liked by others. The hypertensive personality was dominated by excessive but inhibited hostility, which stemmed from conflicts early in life.

After two years of intensive analytic study, Alexander found that these patients were able to gain a great deal of insight about their childhood conflicts. Yet in spite of the insight and moments of catharsis, blood pressure rose unabated as the therapy continued. Quite literally, while the patients were gaining insight and were able to experience ostensible cathartic moments, the entire process appeared to be threatening to kill them. Analytic therapy and catharsis only seemed to make matters worse.

These findings were consistently replicated by a large number of other independent investigators. Indeed the findings were so consistent, that by 1978, when we were first attempted to help a hypertensive professor, it was generally understood that psychotherapy was contraindicated as a treatment modality. (15)

At that time there seemed to be little that could be done to address his problems either in a direct therapeutic manner or in an indirect manner through biofeedback or relaxation.

Psychotherapy and The Decoding of the Human Heart

When we first began to treat the "professor", there was no way to directly or continuously measure blood pressure during the therapy sessions. Thus, during our initial therapy sessions, a nurse would come in every fifteen minutes and measure his blood pressure with an inflatable cuff, stethoscope and mercury manometer. It was a method first developed by N.S. Korotkoff in Leningrad, in 1904, and is still widely used in medicine today. The primary feature that was more or less overlooked was that silence was built into the measurement procedure itself. The doctor or nurse had to listen to the "Korotkoff sounds" in order to measure the blood pressure and this required silence from both the patient and the physician.

With the caveats that had been clearly outlined by Franz Alexander and others, our initial strategy was to avoid any discussion of stressful issues, and if he seemed to get upset, to instruct him to be quiet and breathe deeply. It was, in essence, a strategy of supportive, non-invasive therapy with a strong emphasis on deep breathing. Yet in spite of our efforts to avoid anything that might be emotionally provocative, he seemed to want to discuss his interest in dating a university professor to whom he had been platonically attracted for almost 25 years. Since she was married for all of this time, he never told her about his personal interest. His myocardial infarction occurred shortly after she told him she was very unhappy in her marriage and planned on divorcing her husband. After her divorce, he wanted to ask her out for dinner but was experiencing a great deal of anxiety about that request. By chance, the nurse taking his blood pressure every 15 minutes was approximately the same age as his paramour, and she began to help ease his anxiety. Once he took his paramour out to dinner, his blood pressure began to gradually fall from 185/100 down to a normal range of 130/70. We also suggested that he might begin to consider lowering his BP medications. In essence, over a period of nine months, we had cured the professor without the slightest idea of what we had done that was so efficacious.

Just as we were engaged in terminating our "therapy", I had the good fortune to come across what we affectionately began to call the "green" and then the "blue machines". They were, in fact, the very first prototypes of a computerized way of measuring blood pressure on a minute-to-minute basis, freeing both the patient and doctor to continually talk during the measurement procedure. [16]

With great anticipation, I could scarcely wait until I was able to measure the professor's blood pressure with this computerized device. The results were simply astonishing: when the professor was silent and I was talking, his blood pressure ranged around 135/70 mm Hg. But just as soon as he began to speak, his blood pressure rapidly increased, up to levels around 200/100 mm Hg. The results were so dramatic, and replicated repeatedly during our session, that I immediately assumed the computer machine had to have been defective or inaccurate. The overall conclusion was disconcerting. It seems that we had "cured" the professor only when he was quiet. It also seemed obvious that our intuitive instructions to breathe and be quiet whenever he would begin to talk about stressful issues had proven to be of major benefit to help lower his overall blood pressure.

The first order of business was to check the accuracy of the device. Repeated studies in a coronary care catheter unit quickly revealed that the computer readings perfectly correlated with catheterized measures of blood pressure. A quick screening of fifty laboratory personnel in a protocol that involved three minutes of silence, then two minutes of talking or reading a book aloud, and then three minutes of silence revealed that everyone's blood pressure rapidly and significantly increased as soon as they began to speak or read a book aloud. Within a year, we had shown that there was a direct and linear correlation between basal pressure readings and the magnitude of the pressure increases while talking.

Hypertensive individuals increased their pressure far more than normotensive individuals. There also was a linear correlation with age....older people exhibited far greater increases when they talked than younger people. Even newborn infants could double their blood pressure when they cried, an observation that led to the title of a book on the meaning of these pressure increases, *A Cry Unheard*. [17] We began to sense that we had helped to lower the professor's blood pressure because we had, in part, unwittingly heard his cry and had, so to speak, "mothered" his pressure back down to normal.

The paradox of loneliness-induced premature death and marked increases in blood pressure while talking was impossible to ignore. While *The Broken Heart* asserted that human loneliness ranked among the leading causes of premature death, especially from heart disease, we were now discovering that talking itself could have powerful effects on the human heart. It initially seemed as if one was damned if they were lonely, yet stressed if they tried to talk with others to ease their loneliness.

It also was immediately apparent why the type of psychoanalytically-oriented psychotherapy studied by Franz Alexander had led to ever increasing levels of blood pressure among hypertensive patients; it appeared that talking increased blood pressure in hypertensive patients. That reality could scarcely be ignored. The higher the resting blood pressure, the more it increased when a hypertensive person began to speak. Therapy that encouraged hypertensive patients to continuously talk would inexorably increase their blood pressure throughout the sessions.

Beyond the clarification of a number of therapeutic issues that had previously escaped understanding, additional studies further clarified the magnitude of the pressure increases while talking. Rate and intensity of speech influenced the magnitude of the increases. Breathing patterns also had a major impact. People who tended to talk in a breathless manner increased their pressure far more than individuals with more normal breathing patterns. There were, as well, a number of physiological variables that helped clarify the nature and magnitude of these communicative pressure increases. These included intrapleural pressure, left ventricular ejection fraction, oxygen uptake, and most importantly peripheral resistance. They all contributed in a significant way to pressure increases while speaking. [18] In addition, various neural and humoral variables also played a major role. These were dissected by observations made in heart transplant patients. In spite of having someone else's dennervated heart, and taking strong dosages of antihypertensive medications, these patients also exhibited major increases in blood pressure as soon as they began to talk.

Nor was the phenomenon caused by talking alone, but rather involved the act of communicating. Deaf individuals showed identical blood pressure increases when they used sign language to communicate with others. And hypertensive deaf individuals increased their pressure more than normotensive individuals as soon as they began to sign. [19]

There appeared to be a universal dimension to the blood pressure increases while talking. Everyone exhibited this response, except schizophrenics! Curiously, unlike any other group, schizophrenics consistently lowered their blood pressure when they talked, and whether they were on medications or drug-free did not make any difference. Not only did schizophrenics exhibit abnormally low blood pressure at rest, they also lowered their pressure when they spoke. Ironically, if they complained about something that was incidental, such as the hospital food, they would immediately exhibit marked hypertensive increases in pressure. It almost seemed as if schizophrenics withdrew from communication in order to avoid major hypertensive reactions to talking. [20]

The Effect of Person and the Orienting Reflex Rediscovered in Psychotherapy

Ironically as our research efforts expanded in what seemed to be a dozen directions, our interests also came full circle. We began to wonder whether companion animals could affect the cardiovascular health of human beings in a way that was similar to their cardiac reactions to petting.

In a major epidemiological study of this question, we followed 150 heart patients for over a year after they were released from the University coronary care unit. We were searching for answers about the incidence of morbidity and mortality after they were released from the hospital. What determined who would live and who would die and what were the factors that influenced long-term survival? A large number of physiological, social, economic and pharmacological variables were recorded that potentially played a role. When the results were statistically analyzed, the findings were a great surprise: the single most important factor determining who lived and who died was the extent of damage to the myocardial tissue. The second most important variable, however, was an even greater surprise: those heart patients who did not have an animal as pet were four times more likely to die than those who had a pet. [21] Extending these studies to children, we then observed that a child's resting pressure was significantly lower if a dog was allowed to roam freely in the room. Even more surprising was the fact that when a child touched a dog, or petted a dog, there was an immediate and highly significant lowering of the child's blood pressure. We had indeed come full circle: both the dogs and the children exhibited remarkable lowering of blood pressure to human touch. [22]

This communicative heart appeared to be far more complex than René Descartes'"heater pump". This was a heart in extraordinary dialogue with the world beyond the confines of its own body. There was a hidden dialogical see-saw that was profoundly engaged with the external universe. There was indeed a "Language of the Heart" that was far more than a group of highly sophisticated physiological mechanisms. Aristotle was right! The heart was at the center of it all!

Hearts That Never Forget: Speaking the Unspeakable

While these research studies continued, we also joined a cardiovascular rehabilitation center linked to the Sinai Hospital in Baltimore, Maryland. The American Heart Association had recommended that in order to provide maximal therapeutic benefit to patients in cardiac rehabilitation, three components had to be addressed. These included exercise, diet and stress management. What the American Heart Association failed to define was what comprised "stress" for this group of patients. A simple protocol was devised that included patients being seen at least once for an hour following their exercise on the treadmill.

Their blood pressure was measured automatically each minute on a Dinamap computer while we talked. Every effort was made to avoid stressful topics whenever possible.

Most of these patients were older and experiencing some hardening of their arteries. They were also taking a variety of medications designed to control heart rate, heart rhythm and blood pressure. Almost every patient exhibited far greater pressure increases when they talked versus when they did maximal exercise on the treadmill just before we met. They also exhibited far greater increases in pressure than they did during their preoperative stress test in their cardiologists' office. No medication they were taking effectively blocked pressure increases while talking. In general the diastolic pressure increases while talking were significantly greater than their systolic increases. [23]

There were, in general, marked changes in pressure increases while talking and significant drops in pressure when they were listening to their therapist. Curiously, the greater the increases in pressure, the less likely they were to detect these changes. Very quickly therapy began to take on a rhythmic pattern. As soon as their pressure would increase up to hypertensive levels, I would instruct them to stop talking and breathe deeply. It was also soon obvious that if they could listen to their therapist, pressure would quickly fall back to pre-talking, resting levels. During these 50-minute sessions, it was commonplace to watch both systolic and diastolic pressure readings change 40–50 millimeters of mean mercury even though every effort was made to minimize discussion of stressful topics.

The fact that this population was largely Jewish provided yet another unique circumstance. Perhaps fifty of these patients were survivors of the Holocaust, and had endured brutal experiences as adolescents and as young men and women. Though it might be intuitively obvious, it was nevertheless stunning to watch the pressure increases when they alluded to experiences a half-century earlier. It was not uncommon to observe blood pressure readings of 120/60 suddenly surge to 200/125 when they talked about Buchenwald, or Bergen-Belsen. These rapid pressure surges made it clinically obvious that they would have to stop talking about these traumatic experiences until their cardiovascular system was in a better position to handle the stress. The law was predictable: the higher one's pressure, the more it increased while speaking. Thus, any sustained topic that was leading to pressure surges would only serve to push pressure ever higher. Many patients reported that they anecdotally had never discussed these traumas previously, and their pressure surges when they began to talk made it obvious that these increases in pressure could be life threatening. This led to the concept of "titrating" psychotherapeutic dialogue in a fashion that was physically bearable. Rather than talking in an unending stream of consciousness that threatened to push their blood pressure ever higher, the concept was introduced so that they could only speak about what their hearts could endure.

These hidden pressure surges were, in a somewhat crude analogy, somewhat like human blushing. In any dialogue where one person begins to blush, it is immediately obvious to the other that they are uncomfortable. They might even tell what that blushing means, that one is embarrassed and uncomfortable. In any event, rather than see a person become ever more uncomfortable by blushing, usually the other will try to change the topic. So, too, in therapeutic dialogue, these pressure surges are analogous to a form of hidden internal blushing. It is obvious that when a person's blood pressure rises to clinically problematic levels, every effort should be aimed at first lowering the pressure before continuing the topic.

A Therapeutic Analogy

In summary, talking immediately leads to increases in blood pressure, while looking out, or attending outside of one's self leads to a lowering of blood pressure. It is part of the natural physiological see-saw of human dialogue.

Thus, if one is walking along the peaks of the Blue Ridge Mountains, and looking out at the beauty of the Shenandoah Valley, blood pressure will fall below normal resting levels. Indeed, if in that experience one is not really looking out, but rather taking in the Valley to oneself, it produces a state of intense orienting, which lowers blood pressure. This state is what I call the "Physiology of Inclusion". One literally includes the external world as part of one's physical being.

If one continues on the journey and spots a black bear on the trail, then all those beautiful vistas disappear from one's consciousness, and the body immediately goes into a fight/flight mode of self-preservation. Blood pressure and heart rate begin to surge, and the body prepares itself for survival. This I call the "Physiology of Exclusion".

As human beings we do nothing more frequently than talk. It can exert a profound effect on human health. In an analogous manner, if one is talking to one's mate, when are they perceived as the Shenandoah Valley, and when are they seen as a life-threatening black bear. When talking, do we perceive our mates as something to take in, or exclude from our vision?

The same is true in psychotherapy. It is a continual dialogue, and ought to be designed to facilitate the taking in of information, to relax the body, to lower blood pressure and enhance the dialogue, rather than threatening information, that triggers an unending series of fight/flight responses. Emphasis must be geared towards heightening the Physiology of Inclusion, and thus increasing the body's capacity to relax.

The continual monitoring of the cardiovascular system during therapeutic dialogue gives the therapist information that previously was hidden from our understanding. There is an exquisitely sensitive language of the human heart that we are only now beginning to understand. The mechanistic heart that we inherited from Descartes is in the process of redefinition, moving far closer to the heart that was first outlined by Aristotle—a heart that is at the center of all human dialogue.

References

1. Lynch, J. J. (1985). *The language of the heart: The body's response to human dialogue.* New York, NY: Basic Books.

2. Pavlov, I. P. (1928). *Lectures on conditioned reflex.* (W. H. Gantt, Trans.). New York, NY: International Publishers.

3. Gantt, W. H. (1953). Principles of nervous breakdown-schizokinesis and autokinesis. *Annals of the New York Academy of Sciences, 56,* 143–163; Gantt, W. H. (1966). Reflexology, schizokinesis and autokinesis. *Conditional Reflex, 1,* 57–68.

4. Anderson, S. A., & Gantt, W. H. (1966). The effect of person on cardiac and motor responsivity to shock in dogs. *Conditional Reflex,* 181–189; Gantt, W. H., Newton, J., Royer, F., & Stephens, J. H. (1966). Effect of Person. *Conditional Reflex, 1,* 18–35.

5. Lynch, J. J. & Gantt, W. H. (1968). The heart rate component of the social reflex in dogs: The conditional effects of petting and person. *Conditional Reflex, 3,* 69–80; Lynch, J. J. (1970). The psychophysiology of social attachment.

Journal of Nervous and Mental Disease,151, 231–244; Lynch, J. J., & McCarthy, J. (1967). The effect of petting on a classically conditioned emotional response. *Behavior Research and Therapy, 5*, 55–62.

6. Lynch, J. J. (1967). The cardiac orienting response and its relationship to the cardiac conditional response in dogs. *Conditional Reflex, 2*, 138–152.

7. Thomas, S. A., Lynch, J. J., & Mills, M. E. (1975). Psychosocial influences on heart rhythm in the coronary-care unit. *Heart & Lung, 4*, 746–750; Lynch, J. J., Mills, M. E., Thomas, S. A., & Malinow, K. (1973). The effects of pulse-taking on the cardiac functioning of patients in a coronary care unit [Abstract]. *Psychophysiology, 10*, 200; Lynch, J. J., Thomas, S. A., Mills, M. E., Malinow, K. L, & Katcher, A. H. (1974). The effects of human contact on cardiac arrhythmia in coronary care patients. *Journal of Nervous and Mental Disease, 158*, 88–99; Mills, M. E., Thomas, S. A., Lynch, J. J.. & Katcher, A. H. (1876). Effect of pulse palpation on cardiac arrhythmia in coronary care patients. *Nursing Research, 25*, 378–382; Lynch, J. J., Thomas, S. A., Paskewitz, D. A., Malinow, K. L., & Long, J. M. (1982). Interpersonal aspects of blood pressure control. *Journal of Nervous and Mental Disease, 170*, 143–153; Lynch, J. J., Thomas, S. A., Long, J. M., Malinow, K. L., Friedman, E., & Katcher, A. H. (1982). Blood pressure changes while talking. *Israel Journal of Medical Sciences, 18*, 575–579.

8. Lynch, J. J., Paskewitz, D. A., Gimbel, K. S., & Thomas, S. A. (1977). Psychological aspects of cardiac arrhythmia. *American Heart Journal, 93*, 645–657.

9. Lynch, J. J., Flaherty, L., Emrich, C., Mills, M. E., & Katcher, A. H. (1974). Effects of human contact on the heart activity of curarized patients in a shock-trauma unit. *American Heart Journal, 88*, 160–169.

10. Lynch, J. J. (1977). *The broken heart: The medical consequences of loneliness.* New York, NY: Basic Books.

11. Lynch, J. J., & Paskewitz, D. A. (1971). On the mechanisms of the feedback control of human brain wave activity. *Journal of Nervous and Mental Disease, 153*, 205–217; Lynch, J. J., Paskewitz, D. A., & Orne, M. T. (1974). Some factors in the feedback control of the human alpha rhythm. *Psychosomatic Medicine, 36*, 399–410; Lynch, J. J. (1973). Biofeedback: Some reflections on modern behavioral science. *Seminars in Psychiatry, 5*, 551–562; Lynch, J. J. (1970). The stimulus–the ghost–the response: The carousel of conditioning. *Conditional Reflex, 5*, 133–139.

12. Benson, H., & Wallace, R. K. (1972). Decreased blood pressure in hypertensive patients who practice meditation [Abstract]. *Circulation, 46*(Suppl. II), 516; Benson, H., & Klipper, M. Z. (1975). *The relaxation response.* New York, NY: William Morrow.

13. Wolf, S., Cardon, P. V., Shepard, E. M., & Wolff, H. G. (1955). *Life stress and essential hypertension.* Baltimore, MD: Williams and Wilkins.

14. Ibid #1

15. Ibid #1

16. Ibid #1

17. Lynch, J. J. (2000). *A cry unheard: New insights into the medical consequences of loneliness.* Baltimore, MD: Bancroft Press.

18. Ibid #17.

19. Malinow, K. L., Lynch, J. J., Foreman, P. J., Friedman, E., & Thomas, S. A. (1986). Blood pressure increases while signing in a deaf population. *Psychosomatic Medicine, 48,* 95–101.

20. Ibid #1

21. Friedmann, E., Katcher, A. H., Lynch, J. J., & Thomas, S. A. (1980). Animal companions and one-year survival of patients after discharge from a coronary care unit. *Public Health Reports, 95,* 307–312; Katcher, A. H., Friedmann, E., Beck, A. M., & Lynch, J. J. (1983). Looking, talking, and blood pressure: The physiological consequences of interaction with the living environment. In A. H. Katcher & A. M. Beck (Eds.), *New perspectives on our lives with companion animals.* Philadelphia, PA: University of Pennsylvania Press.

22. Friedmann, E., Katcher, A. H., Thomas, S. A., Lynch, J. J., & Messent, P. R. (1983). Social interaction and blood pressure: Influence of animal companions. *Journal of Nervous and Mental Disease, 171,* 461–465; Thomas, S. A., Lynch, J. J., Friedman, E., Suginohara, M., Hall, P. S., & Peterson, C. (1984). Blood pressure and heart rate changes in children when they read aloud in school. *Public Health Reports, 99,* 77–84.23

23. Thomas, S. A., Freed, C. Friedmann, E., Stein, R., Lynch, J. J., & Rosch, P. J. (1992). Cardiovascular responses of patients with cardiac disease to talking and exercise stress testing. *Heart & Lung, 21,* 64–73.

James J. Lynch, Ph.D. is the author of five books, including The Broken Heart: The Medical Consequences of Loneliness (Basic Books, 1976, translated in 11 languages) "The Language of the Heart: The Human Body in Dialogue, (Basic Books, 1985, Translated into three languages) and A Cry Unheard: New Insights into the Medical Consequences of Loneliness (Bancroft Press, 2000, Trans. into 3 languages).

He is a Board Member of the American Institute of Stress, and the Director of The Life Care Health Center in Baltimore, Maryland. For more than thirty years, he served on the medical school faculties of the Johns Hopkins University, the University of Pennsylvania, and the University of Maryland Medical Schools. He lives with his wife Eileen in Baltimore, MD.

Lynch studied under W. Horsley Gantt, M.D. at the Johns Hopkins Hospital for over a decade. Dr. Gantt was the last American student of Ivan Pavlov. He began his own teaching career as an Instructor of Psychiatry at the Johns Hopkins Medical School in 1965. In 1976 he was appointed full Professor at the University of Maryland Medical School. From 1976 through 1989 he directed the Center for the Study of Human Psychophysiology. Since 1989 he has directed the Life Care Health Center in Baltimore. In 1978 he published the original and seminal work documenting the powerful impact that human dialogue has on regulating human blood pressure, and in 1976 was the first to document the devastating health consequences of human loneliness.

More than 10 Chapters in medical textbooks, Lynch also has published over 100 research articles in peer-reviewed medical journals. He has appeared on over 25 international television programs, on virtually every national television and syndicated news outlet. His "60 Minutes" segments documenting the health benefits of pets have been rebroadcast numerous times. These documentaries helped begin the movement to bring pet animals into nursing homes and hospitals, as well as begin a national movement to utilize pet animals to help children read. His work on the effects that human relationships and human communication exert on cardiovascular health remains the central focus of his research interests and clinical work with heart patients in Phase Two Cardiac Rehabilitation.

Good–Heartedness is Good for Your Heart

Richard Hill

It seems almost weird and perhaps pretentious to suggest that there is science to show that kindness, good–heartedness, positive social engagement and feeling good about yourself is an evolved factor in our capacity to heal, be well and stay well, but this is true. The era of the tough, individual, socially disengaged hero that saves the world is past. The hero/heroine of our health and well being is in the activities that occur between us and the subsequent activities that are generated within us.

Neuropsychobiological science is discovering that our fundamental functionality is dependent on being an engaged, social species. The very development of our brains, our biology, is dependent on interaction with the environment and with other people. Daniel Siegel, developer of Interpersonal Neurobiology, has said that neuroscience is proving the value and importance of kindness to our health and wellbeing (personal communication) and Ernest Rossi has long talked about the benefits of art, truth and beauty in the psychosocial genomic processes of daily life (Rossi, 2004).

We are joined, you and I, by a flow of action and reaction between mechanisms specifically evolved for interpersonal engagement–faces, facial expression, eye contact, gestures and vocal communication (Porges, 2011). Each brain rapidly builds mental maps of the 'other' through a cascade of conscious and non-conscious cues (Siegel, 2007). Mirror neurons form a sense of awareness of physical and movement similarities and intentions before our conscious awareness even begins to reflect (Sinigaglia & Rizzolati, 2011) on the content rich display being transferred across the 'social synapse' (Cozolino, 2006, p.5) between bodies, brains and minds.

If we only existed in our brains and minds, like Putnam's philosophically mischievous *brain in a vat*' (1981, p. 1), then this interplay between brains and minds would be limited to mental mapping process, but we are more—activities above the neck are given numerous pathways to extend the interplay into the biology below the neck. The experience without is the enriching opportunity that can trigger activity within that has the capacity to enable an organism to adapt, change, develop and even promote self generation (Rossi, 1993).

When the experience is positive, safe, pleasurable and socially rewarding, there is a cascade of reaction that transforms the experience into a biological conversation that is very different from the activity that is generated by stress, fear and danger. Of the numerous mechanisms that connect brain and body, the most ardent is arguably the vagus nerve. The vagus nerve is also known as the tenth (X) cranial nerve. It emerges from the lower part of the brainstem (medulla oblongata) and leaves at the base of the skull (jugular foramen), passing close to the jugular and then extends throughout the abdomen, connecting with heart, lungs, stomach, liver, spleen, kidneys, adrenals and intestines (Monkhouse, 2006). Efferent information (from the brain) is conveyed through the vagus nerve more extensively than any other single nerve. There is also afferent information (to the brain) conducted via the vagus nerve (Berthoud & Neuhuber, 2000). It is an important 2-way street (Thayer, 2007).

The activity between the brain and heart through the vagus creates the state of interplay called 'vagal tone'. Good vagal tone is better for health and well being and it is now being shown that good vagal tone is directly related to the quality of experience that is occurring across the social synapse (Fredrickson, 2013). Barbara Fredrickson shows that positive development of the vagal tone changes the rhythm of the heart by refining what is called 'heart rate variability' (HRV). Basically, this is a variation in the frequency of heart beats as you breathe in and out. It is healthier to have a higher rate of variability. Fredrickson tested the quality of vagal tone in relation to a 6 week program of warmth and kindness experiences between participants and toward the self. This resulted in raising vagal tone and positively improving HRV. This experiment showed two important things: firstly, that vagal tone is not fixed and, like brain plasticity, can alter in relation to experience throughout life; and secondly, that vagal tone can be increased through engaging and caring social experience.

The story does not end there, although that was the specific inquiry of Fredrickson's research. Investigating the literature, especially when the scope of relevance is widened, we discover that the benefits are not only cardiovascular, but also in immune system response (Weber et al., 2010; Thayer, 2009). From a simply logical view the immune system uses blood vessels (along with lymph systems and bone marrow) to move about the body (Schwartz, et al., 1981). The better the condition of the heart, the better is the flow of the immune biochemical response around the body. Equally important to blood flow is the condition of blood vessels and the cardiovascular system. Reductions in stress and anxiety are fostered by positive social engagement which reduces levels of cortisol (Uvnas-Moberg, 1998). Lower cortisol levels have a beneficial effect on the cardiovascular system. It is the interplay of these and other systems in our biology that lead to better health. We have worked out the nature and process of these different systems through productive scientific method, but it is important to re-engage them into the interplay that is the true nature of our biology. Having said that, I want to return to the specific processes of the immune system and the vagus nerve.

The need for up or down regulation of inflammatory elements is communicated to the brain from the immune system via the vagus nerve. This is facilitated by the neurotransmitter acetylcholine which acts as a brake to inflammatory processes. Stimulation of the vagus nerve is a therapeutic process that has been found to stop or at least down regulate the production of inflammatory markers by promoting the distribution of acetylcholine throughout the abdomen. This enables the immune system to avoid the hyperactivity that can severely compromise the organism and even cause death (Hansen, et al., 2001). Vagus stimulation is used in the treatment of resistant depression (Nemeroff, et al., 2006) and epilepsy (Ben-Menachem, 2002). There is a calming effect, a regulation of inflammation and a positive effect on HRV.

Vagus nerve stimulation is, however, an invasive treatment that requires applying electrical stimulation to the vagus nerve. We might be well to also think of less acute stimulation as a preventative measure. In our modern, complex environment of chronic stimulation of the immune system (chronic stress, obesity, sedentary excess, environmental pollution, poor diet) it might be reasonable to suggest that improving vagal tone through positive social interaction is beneficial to enhance the responsiveness of the vagus. As we have seen, the benefit of positive social interaction to vagal tone is more than just about HRV. A positive social interaction improves the function of the immune system, reduces inflammation, promotes relaxation and calm and reduces stress and anxiety.

This interplay helps us to understand how positive social engagement creates not only health and wellbeing, but also improves our self healing response and recovery from disease and toxins, whether these toxins are from the external or internal environment. The bottom line is that it is a really good idea to enjoy good company and to seek out those who bring feelings of connection, engagement and a *joie de vivre*. Understanding the biology of the interplay need not diminish our capacity to be surprised and wonder at the outcome. This is important because supporting and encouraging a sense of wonder and a feeling of the tremendous we are able to stimulate brain plasticity and gene expression, especially in the production of brain derived neurotrophic factor (BDNF) which is the necessary building block of brain plasticity (Rossi, 2002).

It may seem unrealistic that so much emerges from the seemingly simple act of enjoying the company of others (Holt-Lunstad, et al., 2010), but that is the nature of complex self-organising systems. Simple actions can have expansive effects on a complex system. This leads us to the point where we should turn our minds to the reverse perspective and discuss the many concerns of a disengaging society, of a chronically stressed culture and so many of the other social problems that interfere with positive social engagement. This social behaviour perspective is, or at least should be, a deep concern for all those concerned for mental health and wellbeing, but for the present, let us ponder on the positive potential of vagal tone through psychosocial activity. We know that going for a vigorous daily walk and eating healthy food are the first prescriptions for many problems like depression. It seems there are also many reasons for us to appreciate that a good heart is a direct result of good heartedness and that good company is like a sweet medication for health and wellbeing.

References:

Ben-Menachem, E. (2002). Vagus-nerve stimulation for the treatment of epilepsy. *The Lancet Neurology,* 1(8): 477-482.

Berthoud, H. R., & Neuhuber, W. L. (2000). Functional and chemical anatomy of the afferent vagal system. *Autonomic Neuroscience, 85* (1–3): 1–17.

Cozolino, L. (2006) *The Neuroscience of Human Relationships*. New York, NY: W.W. Norton.

Fredrickson, B. (2013). *Love 2.0: How Our supreme Emotion Affects Everything We Feel, Think, Do, and Become*. New York, NY: Hudson Street Press.

Hansen M. K., O'Connor K. A., Goehler L. E., Watkins L. R., Maier S. F. (2001) The contribution of the vagus nerve in interleukin-1beta-induced fever is dependent on dose. *American Journal Physiology*, 280: R929-34.

Holt-Lunstad, J., Smith, T. B., & Layton, J. B. (2010). Social relationships and mortality risk: a meta-analytic review. *PLoS Medicine*, 7(7):e1000316. doi: 10.1371/journal.pmed.1000316

Monkhouse, S. (2006) *Cranial Nerves: Functional Anatomy*. Cambridge: Cambridge University Press.

Nemeroff, C. B., Mayberg H. S., Krahl S. E., McNamara J., Frazer A., Henry T. R., George M. S., Charney D. S., & Brannan S. K. (2006). VNS therapy in treatment-resistant depression: clinical evidence and putative neurobiological mechanisms. *Neuropsychopharmacology, 31* (7): 1345–55.

Porges, S.W. (2011). *The Polyvagal Theory*. New York, NY: W.W. Norton.

Putnam, H. (1981) Brains in a vat (Ch. 1, pp. 1-21) in *Reason, Truth and History*. Cambridge: Cambridge University Press.

Rossi, E. L. (1993). *The Psychobiology of Mind-Body Healing*. New York, NY: W.W. Norton.

Rossi, E. L. (2002). *The Psychobiology of Gene Expression*. New York, NY: W.W. Norton.

Rossi E. L. (2004). Art, truth, and beauty: the psychosocial genomics of ocnsciousness, dreams and brain growth in psychotherapy and mind-body healing. *Annals of Psychotherapy and Integrative Health,* Fall 7(3): 10-17.

Schwartz, C., Werthessen, N., & Wolf, S. (1981) The Lymphatic Circulation. *Structure and Function of Circulation, vol 2* (Fifth ed.). New York: Plenum Press. pp. 502–503

Siegel, D. J. (2007). *The Mindful Brain.* New York, NY: W.W. Norton

Sinigaglia, C., & Rizzolatti, G. (2011). Through the looking glass: self and others. *Consciousness and Cognition,* 20: 64–74.

Thayer, J. F. (2007). What the heart says to the brain (and *vice versa*) and why we should listen. *Psychological Topics,* 16(2): 241-250.

Thayer, J. F. (2009). Vagal tone and inflammatory reflex. *Cleveland Clinic Journal of Medicine,* 76(suppl. 2): s23-s26.

Uvnas-Moberg, K. (1998) Oxytocin may mediate the benefits of positive social interactions and emotions. Psychineuroendocrinology, 23(8): 819-835.

Weber, C. S., Thayer, J. F., Rudat, M., Wirtz, P. H., Zimmermann-Viehoff, F., Thomas, A., Pershel, F. H. Arck, P. C., & Deter, H. C. (2010) Low vagal tone is associated with impaired post stress recovery of cardiovascular, endocrine and immune markers. *European Journal of Applied Physiology,* 109(2): 201-211.

Richard Hill, MA, MEd has had an eclectic and fascinating journey to become an internationally recognized speaker and educator on the mind, the brain, psychosocial genomics and the human condition. Richard is a practicing psychotherapist, author and developer of the Curiosity Oriented Approach. He is also the creator and host of the online interview program, MindScience TV.

Heart-Brain Neurodynamics: The Making of Emotions

Rollin McCraty

Emotions are...
the function where mind and body most closely
and mysteriously interact.

—Ronald de Sousa, *The Rationality of Emotion*

As pervasive and vital as they are in human experience, emotions have long remained an enigma to science. This monograph explores recent scientific advances that clarify central controversies in the study of emotion, including the relationship between intellect and emotion, and the historical debate on the source of emotional experience. Particular attention is given to the intriguing body of research illuminating the critical role of ascending input from the body to the brain in the generation and perception of emotions. This discussion culminates in the presentation of a systems-oriented model of emotion in which the brain functions as a complex pattern-matching system, continually processing input from both the external and internal environments. From this perspective it is shown that the heart is a key component of the emotional system, thus providing a physiological basis for the long-acknowledged link between the heart and our emotional life.

The Mental and Emotional Systems

The relationship between mind and emotions has been deliberated at length throughout history, with most schools of thought drawing a boundary between them. Perception, appraisal, arousal, attention, memory, thinking, reasoning, and problem solving are often grouped together under the broader heading of cognition, or the mental system. The emotional system, on the other hand, encompasses feelings, which can span a range of intensity. The importance of gaining a deeper understanding of the emotional system has become increasingly recognized as an important scientific undertaking, as it has become clear that emotions underlie the majority of the stress we experience, influence our decisions, provide the motivation for our actions, and create the textures that determine our quality of life. In recent years, the concept of "emotional intelligence" has emerged, claiming that emotional maturity is as important as are mental abilities in both personal and professional spheres, and that emotional competencies often out-weigh the cognitive in determining success.[1]

The tendency to view emotions as operating separately and apart from rational or intellectual capacities dates back to the times of the ancient Greeks. Thus, historically, thinking and feeling—or intellect and emotion—have often been portrayed as opposing forces engaged in an incessant battle for control over the human psyche. Plato maintained that strong emotions made it impossible for him to think and described emotions as wild horses that had to be reined in by the intellect, while Christian theology has traditionally regarded many emotions as sins and temptations to be overcome by reason and willpower. Traditionally, the intellect was held in high regard, while emotions were considered "irrational" and received little recognition. However, a modern-day examination of emotions presents us with an entirely new perspective, providing a more comprehensive understanding of the emotional system and illuminating the critical roles that emotions play in human experience, performance, and rationality.

Most contemporary researchers agree that cognition and emotion are distinct functions mediated by separate but interconnecting neural systems. A number of research centers, rather than studying these systems in isolation, are attempting to understand the essential dynamic interactions that occur between them. From a neuroscience perspective, several intriguing forms of interaction have been discovered that link the cognitive centers with the emotional processing areas of the brain. For example, bidirectional neural connections that exist between the frontal cortex and the amygdala permit emotion-related input from the amygdala to modulate cortical activity and cognitive input from the cortex to modulate the amygdala's emotional information processing.[2-4]

Beyond these hard-wired neural connections, biochemical bridges also link key components of the mental and emotional systems. The cortex, for instance, has been found to contain a high density of receptors for many neuropeptides that are also heavily concentrated in the brain's subcortical areas, which are associated with emotional processing.[5] Evidence suggests, moreover, that communication channels linking the mental and emotional systems are essential for the expression of our full range of mental capacities.[6]

In his book, *Descartes' Error*, neurologist Antonio Damasio presents evidence that patients with brain damage in the frontal lobes, a key site of integration of the cognitive and emotional systems within the brain, can no longer function effectively in the day-to-day world, even though their intellectual abilities are perfectly intact. Damasio presents a powerful argument supporting the seemingly counter-intuitive position that input from the emotional system to our thought centers not only facilitates, but is actually indispensable to, the process of rational decision-making.[7]

Emotions influence nearly every type of cognitive activity in subtle yet crucial ways. Emotions can direct attention. This phenomenon is known as the *mood-congruity effect*[8] Thus, people in a given emotional state pay more attention to stimuli that are emotionally congruent with their current emotional state. Emotions also influence memory and learning, an effect known in neuroscience as *emotion state-dependent memory.*[9] This is why information learned or obtained in a given emotional state may be more easily retrieved if the individual returns to an emotional state similar to the one that prevailed during the original learning. Emotions can also affect judgment, as well as the cognitive processing style employed during problem solving. This effect is readily demonstrable in the laboratory, as well as in everyday life.[10]

While two-way communication between the cognitive and emotional systems is hard-wired into the brain, the actual number of neural connections going from the emotional processing areas to the cognitive centers is greater than the number going the other way.[4] This goes some way to explain the powerful influence of emotions on thought processes. It also provides insight into how emotional experience, in contrast to thought alone, can often be a powerful motivator of future attitudes and behavior, influencing moment-to-moment actions as well as both short-term and long-term performance. While emotions can easily dispel non-emotional events from conscious awareness, non-emotional forms of mental activity, such as thoughts, do not so easily displace emotions from the mental landscape. Likewise, experience reminds us that the most pervasive thoughts, least easily dismissed, are typically those fueled by the greatest intensity of emotion.

Interestingly, the seventeenth century philosopher René Descartes noted this same point over three hundred years ago. In commenting on the function of human emotion in his *Treatise on the Passions of the Soul*, Descartes wrote:

The utility of all passions consists alone in their fortifying and perpetuating in the soul thoughts, which it is good it should preserve, and which without that might easily be effaced from it. And again, all the harm which they can cause consists in the fact that they fortify and conserve these thoughts more than necessary, or that they fortify and conserve others on which it is not good to dwell.[11] (art. 74)

Descartes' views on emotions were clearly more sophisticated than the simplistic notion that emotions are antagonists to rational thought. Descartes considered emotions a double-sided coin. They give substance and sustenance to what otherwise may have been ephemeral thoughts. As a result, they can work both for and against us. Descartes was really highlighting the contrast between the potential of effectively managed emotions and the harm caused by unmanaged emotions. Whereas effectively managed emotions work in synchrony with the mind to facilitate its activity, unmanaged emotions can be the source of mental chaos.

Mental and Emotional Coherence

To further refine Descartes' premise and express it within the context of the concepts discussed here, we can say that when there is *coherence* within and between the mental and emotional systems, they interact constructively to expand awareness and permit optimal psychological and physiological functioning. Conversely, when the mental and emotional systems are out-of-phase, they lack synchronization and thus interact in a conflicting manner, thereby compromising performance. For example, people commonly tell themselves to "think positive" about a challenging task, yet emotionally they may still dread doing it. When our emotions are not aligned with getting the task accomplished we lack motivation and enthusiasm, which limits our access to creativity and insight, and thus impedes our overall performance. In other words, as many of us have likely experienced, positive thoughts or affirmations are often only superimposed on an underlying internal environment of emotional turmoil. In such cases, "positive thinking" is rarely able to produce an enduring shift in the negative feelings.

To better understand an experience such as this, it is important to realize that many common emotion regulation strategies operate on the assumption that all emotions follow thought, and thus by changing one's thoughts, one should be able to gain control over one's emotions. However, in the last decade, research in neuroscience has made it quite clear that emotional processes operate at a much higher speed than thoughts, and frequently bypass the mind's linear reasoning process entirely.[4] In other words, emotions do not always follow thought; in many cases, in fact, emotions occur independently of the cognitive system and can significantly bias or color the cognitive process and its output or decision.[3, 4]

Since the mind and emotions affect a wide range of abilities and responses, mental and emotional coherence are of the utmost importance. Vision, listening ability, reaction times, mental clarity, problem solving, creativity, and performance in a wide range of tasks are all influenced by the degree of coherence of these two systems at any given moment. Because emotions exert such a powerful influence on cognitive processes, emotional incoherence often leads to mental incoherence. Furthermore, emotional incoherence is often the root cause of "mental" problems and stress. Mental health is maintained by emotional hygiene—emotional self-management—and mental problems, to a large extent, reflect a breakdown of emotional order or stability.

On the other hand, increasing stability in the emotional system can often bring the mind into a greater sense of peace and clarity as well. When the mental and emotional systems are in sync, we have greater access to our full range of potential and a greater ability to manifest our visions and goals, as the power of emotion is aligned with the mind's capacities. Even more intriguing, we can gain more conscious control over this process than previously believed through the application of tools and techniques designed to increase emotional stability. Empirical research on the outcomes of such techniques indicates that increased mental and emotional coherence, in turn, can lead to a higher degree of physiological coherence, manifested as increased efficiency and synchronization in the functioning of physiological systems.[12]

The positive emotion-focused coherence-building techniques developed by the Institute of Heart-Math engage the heart as a point of entry into the psychophysiological networks that underlie emotional experience.[12-14] One of the research focuses of our laboratory over the last decade has been the study of the patterns and rhythms generated in various physiological systems during the experience of different emotions. Through experimenting with numerous physiological measures, we have found that heart rate variability (heart rhythm) patterns are consistently the most dynamic and reflective of changes in one's emotional state. We have demonstrated that positive and negative emotions can be readily distinguished by distinct changes in heart rhythm patterns. Sustained positive emotions are associated with a noticeably coherent (i.e., ordered, smooth, and sine wave-like) heart rhythm pattern, whereas negative emotions are characterized by a jagged, erratic pattern in the heart's rhythms.[15] Moreover, further exploration led us to discover that unhealthy individuals could be greatly facilitated towards improved physical and emotional health through learning how to generate the coherent heart rhythm patterns displayed by healthy, high-functioning individuals.

An important implication of this work, in relation to the ideas developed in this article, is that the rhythmic patterns generated by the heart are not only *reflective* of emotions, but actually appear to play a key role in *influencing* moment-to-moment emotional perception and experience. In short, through its extensive interactions with the brain and body, the heart emerges as a critical component of the emotional system. Before developing this concept further, we place it in perspective by offering a brief historical review of the evolution of scientific thinking about emotions, leading up to a summary of current scientific understandings in this field.

The Source of Emotional Experience: An Evolving Model

Current scientific knowledge regarding the physiology of emotions has its roots in Galenic medicine. Galen's influence on scientific thinking persisted well into the 1800s, with the notion that thoughts ("spirits") circulate in the ventricles of the brain, and emotions circulate in the vascular system. Medical thinking at that time maintained that temperament was determined by four "humors" or secretions: sanguine, choleric, phlegmatic, and melancholic. Modern biomedical research has supplemented this simplistic model with a rich array of endocrine and exocrine hormones, which are invoked in any serious biological discussion of emotion. According to neuropsychologist Karl Pribram, who oversaw the brain research center at Stanford University for 30 years, the retreat from this perspective has been slow and guarded for two reasons: Old theories do not die easily, and there is an aspect of truth to this view.[16] The "spirits" circulating in the ventricles have turned out to be neural electrical activity, and the "humors" flowing through the vascular system, endocrine secretions.

An arguably defining characteristic of emotions is that they involve greater activation of the autonomic nervous system and more conspicuous participation of the body than do mental states. This intimate relationship between emotions and physiology has been expressed for centuries in song, poetry, and prose. Even ordinary conversation pertaining to emotional experiences contains numerous physiological allusions. There is no question that emotions are accompanied by a vast array of physiological changes. This is why people so often tend to describe emotional experiences in physiological terms, such as "My heart was pounding," "My throat went dry," "My blood ran cold," "My skin crawled," "It was gut-wrenching," and "It took my breath away." That these figures of speech have become so engrained in everyday language attests to our experience of emotional states being intricately intertwined with, if not inseparable from, their bodily manifestations.

But is what is the ultimate *source* of emotions—the body or the brain? Do emotions originate as bodily sensations that are then perceived by the brain, or do they originate in the brain as a product of cognitive processes and only then trickle down into the body? This fundamental controversy has formed the core of a lively debate that has raged for over a century, yielding a fascinating and illuminating progression of ideas.

The James-Cannon Debate

In 1884, the debate over the source of emotional experience formally began with a proposal by psychologist-philosopher William James in his seminal article entitled "What is an Emotion?"[17] James believed that emotional experience is not only accompanied by, but actually *arises from* organic changes that occur in the body in response to an arousing stimulus. These physiological signals (*e.g.*, racing heart, tight stomach, sweaty palms, tense muscles, and so on) are subsequently fed back to the brain, and only *then* felt consciously as a true emotion. James proposed that we can sense what is going on inside our body much the same as we can sense what is going on in the outside world. The awareness of the immediate sensory and motor reverberations that occur in response to a perception (*e.g* the pounding heart, the clenched jaw, etc.) is what makes that perception emotional. Thus, the feeling aspect of emotion is dictated by the physiology and not vice-versa. According to James:

> Our natural way of thinking about…emotions is that the mental perception of some fact excites the mental affection called the emotion, and that this latter state of mind gives rise to the bodily expression. My thesis on the contrary is that *the bodily changes follow directly the* PERCEPTION *of the exciting fact, and that our feeling of the same changes as they occur* IS *the emotion* [17] (pp. 189-190)

James maintained that the precise pattern of sensory feedback relayed from the body to the brain gives each emotion its unique quality. Thus, anger feels different from sadness or love because it has a characteristic physiological pattern or signature. James maintained that physiological responses contributing to emotion were "almost infinitely numerous and subtle,"[17] (p. 191) reflecting the nuances of physiology and its emotional counterpart.

In fairness to James, it should be noted that his original premise—that the sensation of bodily changes is a *necessary condition* of emotion—was subsequently oversimplified by many of his contemporaries, as well as by many modern authors.[18] The oversimplification of James' views suggested that emotions are *nothing but* the sensation of bodily changes. In fact, when using the term "perception" in his writings, James did acknowledge the role of interpretation or cognitive appraisal of the exciting stimulus in the initiation of emotional experience. However, he argued that the emotional "feeling" was not a primary feeling directly aroused by appraisal, but rather a secondary feeling indirectly aroused by the organic changes that occurred following the appraisal.

James' perspective was called into question in the 1920s by the prominent experimental physiologist Walter Cannon.[19] Cannon believed that the essential mechanisms of emotion occurred within the brain alone and that bodily responses and afferent input to the brain were not needed to fully experience emotions. He argued, in brief, that bodily feedback, especially from the viscera, was both too slow and not sufficiently differentiated to explain the dynamic range and variety of emotional expression. Though Cannon felt that bodily sensations could not account for differences between emotions, he believed that they nevertheless played an important role in giving emotions their characteristic sense of intensity and urgency.

To support his views, Cannon demonstrated that artificially induced visceral responses alone do not produce emotions and that animals still show "emotional behavior" when feedback from the viscera is surgically eliminated. Of course, here Cannon was forced to rely solely on behavioral evidence to define the parameters of emotion in his animal subjects. In place of the visceral theory, Cannon proposed a brain (thalamic) theory of emotions. He suggested that emotional expression results from the operation of hypothalamic structures, while emotional feeling results from stimulation of the dorsal thalamus. This theory was based on the observation that emotion-like behavior could be elicited in decorticated and decerebrated animals, but not when thalamic structures were ablated as well. Further, a variety of expressive and bodily responses were obtained when the thalamus was electrically stimulated.[20]

In Cannon's view, the thalamus and hypothalamus discharged simultaneously to the body to produce physiological responses and to the cortex to produce emotional experiences. In measuring the amount of time it took for electrical stimulation of the hypothalamus to produce visceral changes, Cannon concluded that these bodily responses were too slow to be the cause of emotions. He saw them rather as the effect, since his measurements suggested that we would already be feeling the emotion by the time these responses occur.

Much of Cannon's experimental research centered on autonomic nervous system (ANS) responses that occur in states of hunger or intense emotion.[21] His research led him to propose the concept of an emergency reaction—the "fight-or-flight response"—to describe a specific physiological response that accompanies any state in which physical energy must be expended. The sympathetic division of the ANS, which he believed to act in a uniform way regardless of how or why it was activated, mediated this response. Cannon held that the visceral changes accompanying emotion were part of this nonspecific arousal, and thus that all emotions had the same ANS signature.

Cannon's arguments won over the weight of scientific opinion of the day, and his view consequently spawned a search for emotional mechanisms in the brain. Others such as Lindsley and Papez built upon Cannon's theory by mapping out additional sub-cortical and limbic structures and communication pathways involved in the brain's emotion-regulating networks.[22, 23] Experimental evidence demonstrated the existence in the hypothalamic region of an energy-conserving or *trophotropic* process working primarily through the parasympathetic branch of the ANS, and a mobilizing or *ergotrophic* system working through the sympathetic branch.[24] It was assumed that the hypothalamus and dorsal thalamus were at the apex of the hierarchy of control of visceral and autonomic functions and were the key to understanding emotional processes.

Neuropsychologist Karl Lashley was the first to criticize this assumption. He pointed out several flaws in the theory by using lesion studies showing that emotional disturbances (on which the Cannon theory was based) could also be observed following lesions elsewhere, such as in the afferent paths in the nervous system or between the forebrain and thalamic structures.[25] He also noted that neither the James nor Cannon theories could account for the dissociation between outward emotional expression and inner feelings, which is a common clinical and experimental observation.

The Limbic Theory

An important breakthrough came in 1937 when James Papez, a professor of neuroanatomy at Cornell University, described a circuit between centers in the brain and suggested that it might constitute the neural substrate for emotion, thus introducing the idea of a circuit or system rather than a single center. He suggested that blockage of information flow at any point along this circuit would cause disorders of emotions. Now known as the *Papez circuit*, this model described the flow of information from the hippocampal formation to the thalamus, then to the cingulate gyrus, and back again to the hippocampal formation.

This was later elaborated on by Paul MacLean, chief of the laboratory for brain evolution and behavior at the National Institute of Mental Health. In the 1950s, MacLean introduced the concept of the *limbic system* to denote the interacting regions of the brain involved in emotional processing.[26, 27] In addition to the areas of the Papez circuit, MacLean included regions such as the amygdala, septum, and prefrontal cortex in the limbic system. Later, he also originated the *triune brain* model, which delineated three functional brain systems that he believed developed successively in response to evolutionary needs.[28, 29] Although MacLean's theory has had little impact on neurobiology, it has become popular in the lay press and with psychotherapists. However, it should be noted that extensive work in comparative neurobiology unequivocally contradicts the evolutionary aspects of his theory.[30]

MacLean believed that emotional experience could be most accurately described as a response to the *composite of* stimuli the brain receives from the external environment, as a result of ongoing perceptions of the outside world, *and* internal sensations or feedback transmitted to the brain from bodily organs and systems. The limbic system came to be viewed as the receiving station or site for the association and correlation of these varied stimuli, being strategically located to correlate every form of *internal* and *external* perception. MacLean also emphasized the importance of memory and provided data showing that the limbic cortex exceeds the neocortex in the turnover of protein, a measure of the demand for new RNA in memory formation.[31]

Here at last was the seat of emotion—the visceral brain. Karl Pribram summed it up with the following:

> The persuasive power of this suggestion is great: Galen, James…, [and] Cannon…are all saved; visceral [bodily] processes are the basis of emotion; and an identifiable part of the brain is responsible for emotional control and experience because of its selective relations with viscera…The path from the "emotions in the vascular system" to "emotions in the forebrain" had finally been completed, and each step along the way freed us from preconceptions popularly current when the step was taken.[16] (p. 16)

Despite its popularity, there are problems with the limbic theory of emotions and it falls heir to the same criticisms leveled against Cannon. The idea of a specific center (*i.e.*, the thalamus) as a privileged site for emotional experience did not hold up; and the same problem arises with relations between the limbic structures and bodily input, and for that matter, the limbic system itself and emotions. For example, it was found that emotional changes can be observed to accompany lesions in parts of the brain other than limbic areas. Further, ablation and stimulation of limbic structures influence problem solving and other cognitive behaviors in selective ways that cannot be attributed to changes in emotion. In fact, obvious and specific "memory" defects follow limbic lesions, while changes in emotions cannot be found.[20] Obviously, the Papez-MacLean theory, like its predecessors, presented only part of the picture.

With the development of newer techniques for electrical brain stimulation, Pribram and others showed that the so-called "limbic" brain regions were under the surveillance and control of the neocortex.[32] Brain structures such as the hippocampus, amygdala, cingulate cortex, septum, thalamus, hypothalamus, and prefrontal cortex came to be viewed as interpreting experience in terms of feelings rather than "intellectualized" representations. It now appears that the whole brain as well as the ascending input from the body, both neurological and hormonal, are necessary in the full experience of emotion.

Memory

An important aspect of emotional experience is memory. The first associations of memory with specific parts of the limbic system appear to have been made in 1900 by the Russian neurologist-anatomist Vladimir Mikhailovich Bekhterev when he observed memory deficits in a patient with hippocampal degeneration.[20] The story of the search for memory is far beyond the scope of this monograph; however; the work of Canadian psychologist Donald Hebb has special relevance to this paper's theme. In 1949, Hebb predicted a form of synaptic plasticity based on temporal activity, which was verified decades later with the discovery of long-term potentiation.[33] Hebb believed that synaptic connections were the material basis of mental associations; however he went well beyond the naïve connectionism theories of that time period in two important respects. First, he argued that an association could not be localized to a single synapse. Instead, neurons were grouped in "cell assemblies," and an association was distributed over their synaptic connections. Secondly, Hebb rejected the concept that input-response behaviors could be explained by simple reflex arcs connecting sensory neurons to motor or output neurons. He believed that sensory stimulation could initiate patterns of neural activity that were maintained by circulation in synaptic feedback loops. This reverberatory activity made it possible for a response to follow a delay that was characteristic of thought. In essence, Hebb argued for a dual-trace mechanism of memory. Reverberatory neural activity was the trace for short-term memory, and synaptic connections were the trace for long-term memory. He hypothesized the conversion of short-term memory into long-term memory by the stabilization of reverberatory activity patterns. Once such an activity pattern was stored, in a redistribution or change in the strength of synaptic connections, it could be recalled repeatedly by an excitation from sensory neurons or from other reverberatory activity patterns occurring in other cell assemblies that provide inputs. In the past fifty years, several aspects of Hebb's theory have been confirmed, while the technology needed to prove or disprove other aspects does not yet exist.

In the 1970s, new insights into the question of what happens in the brain during the time interval between stimulus and response were made possible with the discovery of long-term potentiation. This and the first neural network models of delay activity provided a candidate for Hebb's "reverberatory" activity. For example, it has been demonstrated that certain prefrontal cortex neurons remain active during delays of many seconds and encode information about the preceding stimulus or the impending response. Changes in distribution and strength of synapses have been confirmed, and this aspect of his theory is not in doubt. What remains unknown is whether the delay between stimulus and response is truly due to a reverberatory type of activity, and if so, if the reverberatory activity is stabilized by long-term potentiation. Also, Hebb's concept of only two memory traces may be incorrect, as it is now known that synaptic plasticity involves many processes operating on different time scales.[34]

Current Perspectives on the Nature of Emotion

Most theorists now agree that emotion involves, at the most fundamental level, the registration and interpretation of a stimulus based on memory processes in addition to information from physiological responses and subjective feeling states. In more recent years, attempts have been made to determine the "correct" sequence of these components in the generation of emotional experience. However, when interpretation, subjective feeling, and bodily responses are all considered as *processes*, rather than discrete events or simple input-output relations, the source of a large part of the controversy dissolves.[18]

We find that it is indeed possible to have emotional processing in specific brain areas simultaneously with input from the body to the brain, each building on the other to contribute to the dynamic process of emotion. Recent elucidation of the numerous afferent pathways through which the body transmits signals to the brain and the interaction of this information with higher-level brain processes provides strong support for this perspective. Elmer Green, Menninger Clinic physician and pioneer of the biofeedback approach to treatment of disease, offered an astute summation of this highly debated topic: *"Every change in the physiological state is accompanied by an appropriate change in the mental emotional state, conscious or unconscious, and conversely, every change in the mental emotional state, conscious or unconscious, is accompanied by an appropriate change in the physiological state.*[35]

The remaining element of the controversy, namely the specificity of physiological responses, must now take into account new data revealing that communication between the body and the brain is much more sophisticated and complex than previously imagined. The generation of such data has been made possible, in part, due to the development of more sophisticated recording techniques and instrumentation that more clearly capture the subtleties and complexities of communication between different bodily systems and between the body and brain. In addition, technological advances have enabled us to achieve finer measurements of neuroendocrine and immune activity, thereby offering a wider view into the array of physiological responses at the cellular level that accompany different emotional states.

Before introducing a new model of emotion that synthesizes and further develops many of the perspectives discussed here thus far, a brief review of the role played by activity in both the efferent and afferent pathways of the nervous systems in emotional experience is relevant.

Specificity of Autonomic Responses

Let's return to Cannon's assumption that all emotions are associated with the same basic state of non-specific arousal or activation of the ANS. In the 1960s, Stanley Schachter and Jerome Singer, social psychologists at Columbia University, embraced this view by suggesting that a cognitive interpretation of a basically undifferentiated state of physiological arousal within the social or environmental context of the arousing stimulus was the missing factor in determining the specificity of emotion.[36] Schachter and Singer's model, called the *two-factor theory* proposed that emotions are produced by both feedback from the body and the cognitive appraisal of what caused those responses. In other words, we label the response according to what we think is causing the response. This theory had a profound influence on the thinking on the subject of emotion at the time. However, in the last thirty years the tide has turned, as increased evidence has emerged to indicate that autonomic responses in different emotional states are much more complex than previously assumed, and certainly far from uniform.

In contrast to the thinking in Cannon's day, which attributed emotional arousal to sympathetic nervous system activation alone, we now understand that simultaneous and complex changes in the patterns of efferent activity in both the sympathetic and parasympathetic branches of the ANS are involved in the experience of different emotions. The sensations produced in any given emotional state depend on the extent to which sympathetic effects are balanced by parasympathetic influences; thus sympathetic/parasympathetic balance has become an important measure in psychophysiological research.

Many emotional states are associated with complex patterns of sympathetic/parasympathetic activity in different tissues. For example, in states of aggression and resentment, increased sympathetic discharges occur in the vascular system while parasympathetic discharges predominate in the gastrointestinal tract. Conversely, increased sympathetic activity occurs in both the cardiovascular and gastrointestinal systems in states of fear. Further, autonomic responses vary both quantitatively and qualitatively with the degree of emotional intensity.[37]

A number of experiments conducted in the 1950s provided evidence that different emotions could be differentiated psychophysiologically[38-41] These findings have been confirmed recently.[42-46] For example, in an experiment by Ekman and colleagues at the University of California in San Francisco, subjects experienced different emotional states (happiness, surprise, disgust, sadness, fear, and anger) both by reliving past emotional experiences and by constructing facial prototypes of emotion, muscle by muscle, according to instruction. Specific differences in the autonomic parameters of heart rate, finger temperature, and skin resistance were found among the six different emotions measured. The response patterns differed not only between positive and negative emotions, but also among the negative emotions of disgust, sadness, anger, and fear. These differences were consistent across profession, age, gender, and culture.[43] While this and other research provided convincing evidence of autonomic variation among different emotional states, the variation measured was often small and present in only some of the physiological parameters, or experienced by only a subset of subjects.

A more recent study measuring multiple autonomic parameters showed that six basic emotions (happiness, surprise, anger, fear, sadness, and disgust) could be fully differentiated on the basis of electrodermal variables (skin resistance, skin conductance, and skin potential), thermovascular variables (skin blood flow and skin temperature), and a respiratory variable (instantaneous respiratory frequency).[45] These results clearly support the concept of emotion-specific ANS activity, which can be demonstrated with the aid of careful experimental procedures providing that a sufficient number of autonomic variables are considered.

Individual differences in patterns of autonomic discharge during emotional states have also been identified and associated with personality characteristics. For instance, individuals who have been characterized as "impulsive" personality types display rhythmic bouts of palmar sweat secretion and increases in heart rate even at rest, while in others, little change occurs in these physiological parameters under similar circumstances.[37]

The Importance of Afferent Input

In addition to understanding how complex patterns of efferent autonomic activity correlate to differing emotions, many scientists are beginning to understand the critical role played by the afferent neural signals that flow from the body to the brain. Afferent feedback from bodily organs has been shown to affect overall brain activity and to exert a measurable influence on cognitive, perceptual, and emotional processes.

Physiology textbooks are replete with diagrams that illustrate nervous system pathways from the brain to autonomically innervated organs. However, many of these illustrations do not complete the communication circuit. They frequently omit the extensive systems of visceral afferent fibers, which carry messages from receptors in the body to the brain. The nerve pathways connecting most organ systems to the brain are, in fact, composed of as many afferent fibers as there are efferent connections;[47] while in some visceral nerves, such as the abdominal vagus, up to 90 percent of the fibers are afferent.[48] Remarkably, we now know that the heart sends more neural traffic to the brain than the brain sends to the heart. While afferent pathways were identified during the early years of autonomic research, their study was not emphasized. However, research conducted primarily in the 1950s through the 1970s began to illuminate the importance of afferent input from the thoracic, abdominal, and neck cavities back to the brain—and the effects of this input on brain activity and emotional experience.

One of the earliest contributors to our understanding of the importance of afferent neural traffic was the German internist, Ludwig van Müller. He was particularly interested in the perception of sensory stimuli arising from internal organs and their role in the regulation of different bodily states and sensations.[49] He pointed out, in 1906, that emotions influence heart rate, and conversely, that heart rate influences emotions. For example, he observed that cardiac palpitations can induce emotions.[50]

Early neurophysiological evidence of the influence of afferent input on brain activity dates back to 1929. Tournade and Malméjac, followed by Koch two years later, showed that stimulation of the carotid sinus nerve (contributing afferent fibers which enter the brain stem), or an increase in pressure in the carotid sinus itself, produced a decrease in muscle tone in anaesthetized animals.[51] Koch also demonstrated that by sharply increasing the pressure within the carotid sinus he could inhibit motor activity and induce prolonged sleep. These results were confirmed in later investigations, which showed that distension of the carotid sinus produced marked changes in cortical electrical activity, from low-voltage fast to high-voltage slow waves (characteristic of sleep), and inhibited activity of the pyramidal nerve cells in the motor cortex, which control muscle movement.[51]

In the 1950s, French and Italian neurophysiologists performed a variety of experiments investigating the effects of changes in heart rate and blood pressure on brain activity. Changes in heart rate and blood pressure are detected by receptors in the heart, the aortic arch, and the carotid sinus. Information from these receptors is transmitted to the brain stem via the vagal and glossopharyngeal nerves.[52] In one study, Bonvallet and Allen demonstrated that elimination of the glossopharyngeal and vagal input to the brain resulted in a prolongation of cortical activation and skeletal muscle activity.[53] Then in 1974, French researchers Gahery and Vigier, working with cats, found that stimulating the vagus nerve reduced the electrical response in the cuneate nucleus of the brain to about half its normal rate[54] Since that time, extensive experimental data have been gathered documenting the role played by afferent input in modulating such varied processes as pain perception,[55] hormone production,[56] electrocortical activity, and cognitive functions.[57-59] Animal studies have now demonstrated that a variety of brain regions are involved in the processing of visceral afferent information, including the hypothalamic and thalamic nuclei, amygdala, hippocampus, cerebellum, somatosensory cortex, prefrontal cortex, and insula.[60, 61] Thus, it has become clear that the influence of cardiovascular afferent signals on the brain is far more pervasive than previously considered.

Uncovering conversations between the heart and brain

Among the first modern psychophysiological researchers to systematically examine the "conversations" between the heart and brain were John and Beatrice Lacey.[62] During 20 years of research throughout the 1960s and 1970s, they observed that afferent input from the heart and cardiovascular system could significantly affect *perception and behavior*. Their research produced a body of behavioral and neurophysiological evidence suggesting that sensory-motor integration could be modified by cardiovascular activity.[52, 63-66]

The Laceys' observations directly challenged the "arousal" or "activation" theory proposed by Cannon. In essence, Cannon believed that all of the physiological indicators underlying emotion—heart rate, blood pressure sweating, pupil dilation, narrowing of certain blood vessels, and so on—moved predictably *in concert* with the brain's response to a given stimulus. Thus, Cannon had suggested that when we are aroused, the sympathetic nervous system mobilizes us to fight or flee. In contrast, in quieter moments, the parasympathetic nervous system relaxes our inner systems. Presumably, autonomic responses all increased together when we were aroused and decreased in unison when we were at rest, and the brain was entirely in control of both these processes.

The Laceys noticed that this view of activation as a single dimension only partially matched actual physiological behavior; they observed that all physiological responses did not always move together. As their research evolved, they found that the heart, in particular, seemed to have its own peculiar logic that frequently diverged from the direction of other ANS responses. In essence, the heart seemed to behave as if it had a mind of its own. In laboratory studies of reaction time and operant responses, the Laceys observed that in response to certain stimuli, all autonomic variables recorded did not exhibit the expected response pattern typical of arousal. At times, for example, heart rate decelerated and blood pressure *decreased*, while simultaneously recorded parameters such as skin conductance, respiration rate, and pupillary dilation all increased as expected. The Laceys called this phenomenon *directional fractionation* and noted that it appeared to be dependent upon the nature of the stimulus and the type of mental processing involved.[63]

The Laceys found that tasks requiring mental concentration or attention to *internal* stimuli (*e.g.* mental arithmetic, reverse spelling, or making up sentences) produced an acceleration in heart rate and an increase in skin conductance. In contrast, tasks requiring attention to the external environment (*e.g.*, detecting colors and patterns or empathizing with a dramatic recitation) produced a marked deceleration in heart rate, although skin conductance still increased. The Laceys also showed that patterns of physiological responses were affected as much by the context of a specific task and its requirements as by emotional stimuli. Thus, heart rate, for example, tends to decrease, even in the presence of a distressing emotional context, when subjects are attending visually or auditorially to events in their external environment; on the other hand, heart rate accelerates when subjects mentally recall and think about the very same unpleasant emotional material.[63-65] Subsequent research also revealed an intriguing link between the heart rate response (but not other autonomic responses) to different environmental stimuli and an individual's cognitive style, or attitude toward the external environment.[67-68]

The selectivity of the heart's response indicated that *it was not merely mechanically responding to an arousal signal from the brain*. Even more intriguing, in simple reaction time experiments, which required attention to external cues, an *anticipatory* deceleration in heart rate was observed during the preparatory interval, and subjects' reaction times were faster during periods when their heart rate was slowing.[52] This led the Laceys to propose that cardiovascular afferent feedback to the higher brain centers plays a role in *facilitating either the intake or rejection of environmental stimuli*, in accordance with the nature of the mental processing required for a given task.[66] In brief, such a mechanism would permit us effectively to "tune out" potentially disruptive external environmental events when performing tasks requiring internal cognitive elaboration, and, conversely, to focus in on external inputs when our activities demanded close attention to our environment.

To support this hypothesis, the Laceys and others found evidence that in humans under normal physiological conditions, brain activity varies in relation to cardiovascular events.[52, 69] Thus, increased heart rate and the resulting increased afferent discharge inhibits (desynchronizes) cortical activity. Conversely, decreased heart rate occurring prior to sensory intake promotes cortical facilitation and processing by reducing brain inhibition.[66] In their reaction time experiments, the Laceys discovered that the greater the cardiac deceleration, the greater the cortical activation, and the greater the behavioral efficiency (*i.e.*, the faster the speed of response). In other words, *afferent input to the brain from the heart can either inhibit or facilitate the brain's activity, which, in turn, can affect perception and motor activity*

Evoked potential studies

A useful technique for the study of how and where information flows through the brain is evoked potential analysis. Evoked potentials (also sometimes referred to as event-related potentials) are obtained using signal averaging, a procedure for separating a known repetitive signal from other signals.

Evoked potential analysis can be used to study the flow of information through many different pathways in the brain. Common applications of the technique are to study the visual, auditory, and somatosensory systems. In the case of the visual system, for example, the flow of information through the nervous system produced in response to a series of light flashes or a changing visual stimulus of any kind can be traced through the different visual pathways as it is processed. In this case, the resulting waveforms are called visual evoked potentials. It is also possible to examine the flow of afferent input through the brain from many other sensory systems, such as the auditory and tactile systems, or to assess how a change in afferent signals generated by one system affects the processing of information in another system.

For example, the effects of cardiac afferent input on sensory perception have been studied by looking at how these signals affect processing in the visual system. It has been shown that the processing of visual information is significantly changed as heart rate and carotid pressure change. These findings provide confirmation of the Laceys' earlier behavioral evidence that cardiovascular activity influences sensory intake.[70]

While these data indirectly support the view that cardiovascular afferent information interacts with higher central nervous functions, experiments by the German researcher Rainer Schandry and others have provided more direct psychophysiological evidence for this perspective. Their work has demonstrated that cardiovascular events like heartbeats are detectable as a signal in the EEG and evoke cortical responses analogous to "classical" sensory event-related potentials.[60, 71, 72] When the heart's afferent signals are being studied, the ECG R-wave is used as the timing source for the signal averaging and the resulting waveforms are called heartbeat evoked potentials (HBEPs). These experiments have shown that the processing of afferent input from the cardiovascular system is accompanied by specific electrical activity in the brain. This processing of cardiovascular afferent information is most pronounced at the frontocortical areas, a brain region known to be particularly involved in the processing of visceral afferent information. Recent findings have demonstrated that the HBEP is significantly diminished in diabetic patients with autonomic neuropathy, and reduced amplitude of the HBEP is significantly correlated with reduced awareness of body sensations.[73] In other words, when the communication of afferent signals from the heart to the brain is compromised, there is less awareness of feeling sensations in the body.

Furthermore, psychological factors, such as motivation, attention to cardiac sensations, and general perceptual sensitivity, have been found to alter HBEPs in the brain in a manner analogous to the cortical processing of external stimuli.[60, 72] These findings confirm our own data demonstrating that focusing attention in the area of the heart and generating a positive emotion alters HBEPs, thus indicating an modulation of cortical processing. Taken together, these data suggest that perception and processing of information arising from bodily processes is comparable to perception and processing of external events, and the effects of both sources of input on perceptual and emotional experience must be considered.

In summary, evidence now clearly demonstrates that afferent signals from the heart significantly influence cortical activity. Specifically, we now know that afferent messages from the cardiovascular system are not only relayed to the brain stem to exert homeostatic effects on cardiovascular regulation, but also have separate effects on aspects of higher perceptual activity and mental processing. Furthermore, as discussed next, there are now data from both animals and humans to support the premise that central *emotional processing* is also altered by afferent input from the heart.

Afferent input influences emotional processing: The role of the amygdala

The influence of cardiovascular afferent input to the brain on emotional processes is highlighted by recent evidence suggesting that psychological aspects of panic disorder are often created by unrecognized paroxysmal supraventricular tachycardia (PSVT), a sudden-onset atrial arrhythmia. According to one study, DSM-IV criteria for panic disorder were fulfilled in more than two-thirds of patients with these sudden-onset arrhythmias. In those patients in whom PSVT was unrecognized at initial evaluation, symptoms were attributed to panic, anxiety, or stress in 54 percent of the cases. In the majority of cases, once the arrhythmia was recognized and treated, the panic disorder disappeared.[74] Interestingly, this study confirmed the observations of pioneer ANS researcher Müller, who reported the induction of emotions by cardiac palpitations over 90 years earlier.[50] Likewise, our research has also shown that changing the pattern of afferent information generated by the cardiovascular system can significantly influence perception and emotional experience.[12, 75]

The amygdala has been the subject of intense scrutiny in recent years. This brain center plays a key role in emotional memory, emotional processing, and dreaming.[76] Several studies have investigated the effects of cardiovascular afferent input on the amygdaloid complex (*i.e.*, the amygdala and associated nuclei). For example, in cats, spontaneous neural activity in the central nucleus of the amygdala has been shown to be synchronized to the cardiac cycle and to be modulated by afferent input from the aortic depressor and carotid sinus nerves.[77] Similarly, data from humans undergoing surgery for epilepsy demonstrated that cells within the amygdaloid complex specifically responded to information from the cardiac cycle.[78] Pribram, who did much of the original mapping of the functions of the amygdaloid complex, found it has extensive projections to both the brain stem autonomic nuclei and the higher cognitive centers, and is thus uniquely placed to coordinate affective, behavioral, immunological, and neuroendocrine responses to environmental stimuli.[16,79] The observed interaction of afferent cardiac input with this brain region supports the view that visceral information not only influences emotional processing and emotional experience, but can also influence hormonal and immune responses.[75]

Taken together with the demonstrated role of the amygdala in the regulation of viscero-autonomic activity and the resultant effects on familiarization, considered below, a new view of emotional processing and regulation emerges.

The Role of Familiarization in Emotional Processing

To further unfold our understanding of the emotional system and the heart's role in emotion, we now review the model of emotion first developed by Karl Pribram.[80] Simply said, in Pribram's model a set of memories, or stable patterns of activity, is formed and maintained in the neural architecture of the brain as we gain experience both in internal self-regulation and in interacting with the external environment. These stable patterns are updated and modified as we encounter new experiences and learn how a certain action usually leads to specific result. All ongoing or current sensory input to the brain, from both the internal and external sensory systems, is compared to these stable patterns. When a mismatch between current input and a stable pattern occurs, novelty is sensed.

These stable patterns create a set of "expectancies" against which breathing, eating, drinking, sleeping, alerting, sexual, and other behaviors are evaluated. The stable neurological pattern acts as a set point against which an input is matched, and therefore determines what is familiar and what is novel, and perhaps exciting.

The set point, based on previous experience, becomes a reference point for evaluating current and future experience, and is biased or adjusted according to ongoing experience. To maintain stability as we encounter life's events, we must make adjustments that return us to the "familiar" set point. These adjustments require us to take an "action"—which can be either an outward action (i.e., control of some kind over the external environment) or an internal adjustment (i.e., self-control of our inner environment). Since our psychophysiological systems are designed to maintain stability and resist change, returning to familiar set points gives us a sense and feeling of security, while remaining in unfamiliar territory causes unrest. Interestingly, this is true even if the established set point is one of chaos and confusion.

Attention

No conscious awareness of anything, including our emotions, is possible until it has captured our attention. Sensory neurons in our eyes, ears, nose, and body are in continuous action, day and night, whether we are awake or asleep. The brain receives a steady stream of information about all the events the sense organs are capable of detecting. It would be bewildering if we were continuously aware of all the incoming information. In fact, we completely ignore most of the information arriving at the brain most of the time. Yet any input is capable of shifting and dominating our attention. In order for this process to function, there must be mechanisms and processes that direct *selective* attention. The attention mechanisms must continuously scan the available information and assign priority, usually based on biological importance. Large, sudden, novel occurrences typically have the ability to grab our attention. Emotions also have the ability to capture and focus attention, and attention is involved in the management of our emotional state.

In 1890, William James described attention thus:

> Everyone knows what attention is. It is taking possession of the mind, in clear and vivid form, of one out of what seems several simultaneously possible objects or trains of thought. Focalization, concentration of consciousness, are of its essence. It implies withdrawal from some things in order to deal effectively with others, and is a condition which has a real opposite in the confused, dazed, scatterbrained state...[81] (pp. 403-404)

Many laboratories around the world have investigated the brain structures involved in awareness and attention. Generally there have been two approaches to attention research: (1) recording physiological or behavioral responses against a background of regular, repeating sensory events and (2) pairing of the outcome of the response to sensory events.

When a new stimulus is presented to the brain, a change in activity in the central and autonomic nervous systems is produced. If the response is short-lived (1–3 seconds), it is called *arousal orienting reflex*. If, however, the stimulus or event is recurrent, the brain rapidly adapts and we *habituate*. For example, people who live in a noisy city adapt to the ambient noise and eventually become unaware of it. However, when they take a trip to the quiet countryside, the lack of noise seems strange and noticeable. Thus, any change in the stimulus will cause the reappearance of the arousal response, or the orienting reflex. The arousal reaction therefore reflects a *mismatch* between the new information and the familiar representation stored in the brain. A change in brain potentials can be measured during the arousal response to a novel stimulus, and is called *mismatch negativity*[82] The observed changes in the nervous system can be separated into a *phasic* component, which habituates quickly, and a long-lasting *tonic* component, which habituates more slowly.[83]

James, and more recently Pribram and McGuiness, also distinguished two types of attention. Pribram and McGuiness called these involuntary and voluntary. *Involuntary primary attention* as James called it, is provoked by certain classes of stimuli that are novel, salient, or intense, which impinge upon our awareness regardless of ongoing activity. *Voluntary attention*, on the other hand, describes the process whereby the individual voluntarily determines the contents of his/her own awareness and the duration of focus. In the Pribram and McGuiness model, the distinction between involuntary and voluntary attention identifies two aspects of attentional control: one regulates *arousal* resulting from a mismatch in sensory input; the other controls the preparatory *activation* of potential responses. In addition, there is a third aspect of attention that serves to coordinate involuntary arousal and voluntary activation, and this aspect of attention requires effort.[2]

Pattern-Matching and the Maintenance of Stability

In their book *Plans and the Structure of Behavior*, Miller, Galanter, and Pribram propose that in order for an organism to maintain continued stability, it must be able to maintain a match between its current experience or "reality" and its neural and hormonal set points and *programs*[84] These programs consist of hierarchies of nested neural feedback loops that maintain memories of familiar experiences, responses, and outcomes. Incongruities or differences in the input (new experiences) arouse or activate us depending upon the degree of mismatch, and, in most cases, determine what action is needed to reestablish stability. When the differences (mismatch) are of sufficient magnitude, there is a temporary discontinuity; importantly, *it is this discontinuity or mismatch—effectively a <u>departure from the familiar</u>—that gives rise to the experience of emotion.* In this context, it is interesting to note that the word "emotion" derives from the Latin *emovere*, which means "to move out or away from."

Pribram, in his book *Languages of the Brain* carries the theory further. When the input to the brain does not match the existing program, an adjustment must be made in an attempt to achieve control and return to stability. One way to re-establish control is by taking an outward action. We are motivated to eat if we feel hungry, run away or fight if threatened, do something to draw attention to ourselves if feeling ignored, etc. Alternatively, we can re-establish stability and gain control by making an internal adjustment (without any overt action). For example, a confrontation at work may lead to feelings of anger, which can prompt inappropriate behavior (*i.e.*, outward actions such as yelling, hitting, etc.). However, through internal adjustments, we can self-manage our feelings in order to inhibit these responses, re-establish stability, and maintain our job.

Thus, stabilization is achieved through external action on the environment or through internal self-control. These processes are referred to, respectively, as motivational control and emotional control. Ultimately, when we achieve stability through our efforts, the results are feelings of satisfaction and gratification. By contrast, when there is a failure to achieve stability or control, feelings such as anxiety, panic, annoyance, apprehension, hopelessness, or depression result.

Pribram and many others have conducted numerous experiments providing evidence that these sorts of internal adjustments, although commonplace, represent a complex interplay between peripheral and central processes. For example, the afferent input systems and even their receptors are modulated by the central nervous system, which alters information processing in the sensory input channel.[86] In other words, the higher brain centers can inhibit or "gate" the information flowing into the brain. There are many examples of how we can control input channels. Where we focus our attention has a powerful effect on modulating inputs and thus on determining what gets processed at higher levels. In a noisy room filled with many conversations, we have the ability to tune out the noise and focus on a single conversation of interest. In a like manner, we can modulate pain from a stubbed toe or headache or desensitize ourselves to sensations like tickling.

Arousal

There is ample support that arousal, measured as EEG desynchronization, occurs in response to novel or unfamiliar input, and that arousal is one of the elements of emotional experience. In classical models of arousal theory, the amount of neural and/or hormonal activity generated in response to a given stimulus or event determines whether the experience leads to familiarization or disruption. Arousal theory states that a correlation exists between the amount of a specific hormone or amount of neural excitation and the amount of emotional arousal.

However, this is only part of the story. Arousal can at times be associated with an increase the *amount* of neural activity, but arousal can also occur without any increase in neural activity. In the latter case what does change, instead, is the *pattern* of activity in the nervous system (for example, variations in the time intervals between sequential firings of a neuron or group of neurons, or in which efferent pathways are active). Therefore, the amount of neural activity does not always necessarily indicate the level of arousal.[80] This is an important realization, as it shifts the focus from thinking in terms of amount of activity alone to understanding the importance of the pattern of activity. This is also related to the observation that differing emotions are reflected in the patterns of the heart rhythm. For example, during an emotional state shift, the *pattern* of beat-to-beat heart rate variability can shift dramatically, while the *amount* of variability remains exactly the same. This is not to imply that changes in the amount of neural activity or amount of heart rate variability are not also important sources of information that contribute to ongoing emotional experience. However, in the broader context of the model presented here, such variations can also be considered as changes in pattern relative to a familiar baseline or set point.

The Role of the Heart

Monitoring the alterations in the rates, rhythms, and patterns of afferent traffic is a key function of the cortical and emotional systems in the brain. Pribram was well aware of the influence of afferent input from the heart and other organ systems in determining the set points, or what becomes the familiar pattern, as far back as 1969, when he wrote:

Visceral feedback constitutes, by the nature of its receptor anatomy and diffuse afferent organization, a major source of input to this biasing mechanism; it is an input which can do much to determine set-point. In addition, cardiovascular and autonomic events are repetitiously redundant in the history of the organism. They vary recurrently, leading to stable habituations; this is in contrast to external changes which vary from occasion to occasion. Habituation to visceral and autonomic activity makes up, therefore, a large share…of the stable base-line from which the organism's reactions can take off.[80] (p. 322)

These set points establish a background against which blood pressure, hormonal balance, and all regularly recurring behaviors are initiated and maintained. For example, when we sense a mismatch between our actual heart rate and the habituated heart rate, we generate a feeling (*e.g.*, excitement or anxiety if heart rate is accelerated). The specific feeling experienced may reflect the nature of the mismatch. Importantly, a mismatch may be registered not only due to changes in heart rate but also due to changes in the pattern of the afferent traffic.

Although input originating from many different bodily organs and systems is involved in the processes that ultimately determine emotional experience, it has become clear that the heart plays a particularly important role. The heart is the primary and most consistent source of dynamic rhythmic patterns in the body. Furthermore, the afferent networks connecting the heart and cardiovascular system with the brain are far more extensive than the afferent systems associated with other major organs. Additionally, the heart is particularly sensitive and responsive to changes in a number of other psychophysiological systems. For example, heart rhythm patterns are continually and rapidly modulated by changes in the activity of either branch of the ANS, and the heart's extensive intrinsic network of sensory neurons also enables it to detect and respond to variations in hormonal rhythms and patterns.[87] In addition to functioning as a sophisticated information processing and encoding center,[88] the heart is also an endocrine gland that produces and secretes hormones and neurotransmitters.[89-92] Thus, with each beat, the heart not only pumps blood, but also continually transmits dynamic patterns of neurological, hormonal, pressure, and electromagnetic information to the brain and throughout the body.[93] Therefore, the multiple inputs from the heart and cardiovascular system to the brain are a major contributor in establishing the dynamics of the baseline pattern or set point against which the "now" (current input) is compared.

The repeating rhythmic patterns generated by the heart, whether they are ordered or disordered, become familiar to the brain. At the brain stem level, these patterns are compared to set points that control blood pressure, affect respiration rate, and gate the flow of activity in the descending branches of the autonomic system. From there, these signals cascade up to a number of subcortical centers, such as the thalamus, hypothalamus, and amygdala, which are involved in the processing of emotion. With the understanding that the emotional system operates essentially as a pattern recognition system, the finding that a significant proportion of people diagnosed with panic disorder actually have an unrecognized atrial arrhythmia is easily understandable. When a sudden-onset arrhythmia occurs, there is a large and sudden change in the pattern of afferent signals arriving at the amygdala and hippocampus, resulting in a significant mismatch between the current input and the familiar, stable pattern. The system is unable to achieve stability through an outward action or through an internal adjustment; the mismatch therefore captures attention and gives rise to feelings of fear and anxiety, which build to panic. In cases where the arrhythmia is constant or occurs more frequently, the system adapts or habituates––in other words, the new input pattern becomes familiar.

On the other hand, a change in the pattern of afferent cardiovascular input that accompanies a more coherent or ordered heart rhythm, such as those that occur with certain breathing techniques or the use of HeartMath positive emotion-focused tools, results in a "pattern match" associated with security and positive emotional experience. These coherent rhythms are familiar to a "healthy" system as they have occurred spontaneously many times during sleep and positive emotional states. However, in many individuals, a coherent pattern is rare and relatively unfamiliar to the brain. In this case, with the practice of self-generating coherent rhythms, they become the familiar baseline pattern and that which the system attempts to maintain.

Emotional Instability

When the neural systems that maintain the baseline reference patterns are in an unstable state (due to stress, anxiety, chemical stimulants, etc.), sensory input from either internal or external sources that would ordinarily be processed smoothly can be perceived as a mismatch and give rise to an uncomfortable feeling. Thus, patterns of neural activity in the brain can effectively predispose the individual towards either stability or instability. The reference patterns can be temporarily destabilized by large, sudden changes in the pattern of afferent activity, such as those that occur in the example of a sudden onset arrhythmia or during an emotionally charged situation. If a reference pattern is destabilized, a mismatch can be perceived even in the absence of novel input. This explains why we can have an upsetting interaction with our spouse, and even though things may have been smoothed over and the event consciously forgotten, we could subsequently be set off by what we perceive as a funny look from a co-worker upon arriving at the office. Physiologically, the instability is still in our system. Under normal circumstances, the look would have gone unnoticed. Likewise, had we been able to stabilize our neural systems by clearing the emotional residue on the way to work, the look from the co-worker would not have thrown us off.

In addition to processes that monitor the input and controls for maintaining stability (pattern matching) in the here-and-now, there are also matching processes that appraise the degree of congruity or incongruity between the past and the now and between the now and the projected future. Furthermore, these prospective appraisals can be divided into optimistic and pessimistic.[94] If the appraisal does not result in a projected ability to return to stability, feelings of fear and anxiety can result. This appraisal could be due to past experience of similar situations or a lack of experience in the projected future situation. However, as we encounter novel situations and learn that we are able to maintain stability, we can apply that experience to similar future situations without fear.

Pribram states that when a homoeostatic system becomes stabilized and a new pattern has become familiar, new sensitivities develop and different strategies and programs are added to handle the acquired sensitivities.[95] In essence, we mature. Encountering novel situations or obstacles requires that we develop new strategies: we either take an external action to gain control or self-manage our internal systems. Once we learn how to handle the new challenge effectively and maintain stability, the strategy (complex pattern) for dealing with the challenge becomes familiar and part of our repertoire. Through this process, we increase our internal self-control and management of emotions as well as our ability to effectively deal with external situations.

The baseline patterns maintained in the neural architecture are modified by other sources of neural and hormonal input that affect the "bias" or sensitivity of the system. Because the neural systems involved in comparing the incoming sensory information are made up of short, fine fibers with many branches, they are especially sensitive to hormonal influences. Thus, the system is readily affected by changes in the patterns of hormonal input associated with different psychophysiological states. In this way hormones provide important influences on the brain processes involved in the experience of emotion.

The Making of Emotions: A Converging View

In summary, we can see earlier theories of emotion, coupled with current research, converging into a more complete and comprehensive view of emotions. Endocrine research significantly advanced the previous view of emotions as "humors." The visceral theory acknowledged an arousal mechanism that provides feelings of interest, novelty, and familiarity, as well as more painful disruptions of stable states. James emphasized the communication of bodily responses to the brain. Cannon's thalamic theory contributed by offering evidence of the thalamus as a prime locus for processing emotional information from the body's chemical homeostatic systems. Papez and MacLean introduced the idea of emotional circuits and systems instead of a single center and added the possibility of a memory component to the emotional system. With Pribram's cortical control of afferent input and monitoring of a departure from stable, familiar patterns, it becomes clear that *both the brain and the entire body are involved in the full experience and expression of emotions*

With this understanding in mind, we can view the experience of emotion as emerging from an intricate array of interactions occurring within a complex system. Broadly speaking, its main components include the brain and nervous system, the hormonal system, and body. Although there are numerous sources of bodily input to the brain, the heart is given particular relevance in the emotional system due to its unique degree of afferent input and its consistent generation of dynamic rhythmic patterns that are closely coupled with changes in emotional state. From a generalized perspective, one of the ways an emotion is generated is through the comparison of information received from the external sensory systems, (*e.g.*, sights, sounds, and smells) against pre-existing memories. This processing occurs at unconscious levels, unless attention is captured, and results in changes in the patterns of descending autonomic activity flowing to the body. This leads to a wide variety of specific changes in biochemical outputs and biophysical states, such as alterations in patterns of muscle tension (especially in the face), adrenal secretions, vascular resistance, cardiac output, and heart rhythms. These alterations, in turn, result in changes in the afferent inputs from the body back to the brain, which are then compared to a set of pre-existing reference patterns. This ascending bodily input is crucial to the felt experience of an emotion, and may or may not reinforce the cognitive level appraisal and labelling of the feeling. The process continues as the system makes external and internal adjustments in order to maintain stability, and, depending upon the outcome, can further color and add textures to the emotional experience. Of course, this is only one example, as the process can also be initiated by changes in the internal systems alone as well as through many combinations of the internal and external sensory systems' interactions with the reference patterns and memories.

Within the context of the model of emotion developed here, we can also gain new insight into the mechanisms underlying the efficacy of the HeartMath emotional restructuring techniques, which produce a positive emotion-driven shift in the heart's rhythmic patterns, and thus a change in the pattern of cardiac afferent input to the brain. The coupling of a more organized pattern of afferent input with an intentionally self-generated positive emotion reinforces the natural conditioning between the coherent physiological mode and the positive emotion. This subsequently strengthens the ability of a positive emotional shift to initiate a physiological shift towards increased coherence, and a physiological shift to facilitate the experience of a positive emotion.

From the perspective presented in this article, HeartMath interventions affect several aspects of the emotional process. First, by reducing nervous system chaos, they stabilize the neural systems that maintain the baseline or reference patterns against which incoming information is compared. They also modify the baseline patterns by reinforcing the coherent psychophysiological patterns associated with positive emotions and allowing these patterns to become familiar, thus effectively establishing a new baseline or norm. Once this new reference pattern established, the system then automatically strives to maintain this state.

With practice of these techniques, as the neural architecture comes to recognize the patterns associated with coherent heart rhythms as familiar, it becomes progressively easier to intentionally generate coherent rhythms and their psychophysiological benefits, even during experiences of stress or challenge. Moreover, we have demonstrated that as people continue to practice intentionally self-generating states of psychophysiological coherence using heart-based techniques, they also begin to demonstrate a greater frequency of *spontaneous* heart rhythm coherence, without conscious use of the interventions. These data support the concept the techniques facilitate an actual re-patterning process at the level of the neural architecture, which can be objectively assessed using electrophysiological measures.

In sum, consistent use of heart-based positive emotion-focused techniques reinforces existing neural pathways that the brain uses to control its input (self-manage) and facilitates the establishment of new control pathways, thus improving our ability to self-manage our emotions and regulate our physiological state. Experientially, the occurrence of a system-wide re-patterning process with consistent use of the HeartMath interventions is supported by reports from thousands of individuals who have noted enduring improvements in many aspects of health, well-being, and performance, increased emotional stability and new capabilities for dealing with stress and challenges. In a very real sense, we become the architects of our own neural landscape.

Acknowledgments
I would like to express my appreciation to Dr. Karl Pribram for his careful review of this monograph and his insightful input on its content.

References

1. Goleman D. *Working with Emotional Intelligence* New York: Bantam Books, 1998.
2. Pribram KH, McGuinness D. Arousal, activation, and effort in the control of attention. *Psychological Review* 1975;82(2):116-149.
3. LeDoux JE. Cognitive-emotional interactions in the brain. In: Ekman P, Davidson RJ, eds. *The Nature of Emotion: Fundamental Questions*. New York: Oxford University Press, 1994: 216-223.
4. LeDoux J. *The Emotional Brain: The Mysterious Under- pinnings of Emotional Life*. New York: Simon and Schuster, 1996
5. Pert CB, Dreher HE, Ruff MR. The psychosomatic network: Foundations of mind-body medicine. *Alternative Therapies in Health and Medicine* 1998;4(4):30-41.
6. Damasio AR. *The Feeling of What Happens*. Orlando, FL: Harcourt, 1999.
7. Damasio AR. *Descartes' Error: Emotion, Reason and the Human Brain*. New York: G.P. Putnam's Sons, 1994.
8. Bower GH. Mood-congruity of social judgements. In: Forgas J, ed. *Emotions and Social Judgements*. Oxford: Pergamon, 1990.
9. Bower GH. How might emotions affect learning? In: Christianson SA, ed. *The Handbook of Emotion and Memory: Research and Theory*. Hillsdale, NJ: Lawrence Erlbaum, 1992: 3-31.
10. Clore GC. Why emotions are felt. In: Ekman P, Davidson RJ, eds. *The Nature of Emotion: Fundamental Questions*. New York: Oxford University Press, 1994: 103-111.
11. Descartes R. *Treatise on the Passions of the Soul* In: Haldane E, Ross G, trans. *The Philosophical Works of Des- cartes*. Cambridge: Cambridge University Press, 1649.

12. McCraty R, Childre D. *The appreciative heart: The psychophysiology of positive emotions and optimal functioning.* Boulder Creek, CA: HeartMath Research Center, Institute of HeartMath, Publication No. 02-026, 2002.

13. Childre D, Martin H. *The HeartMath Solution* San Francisco: HarperSanFrancisco, 1999.

14. Childre D, Rozman D. *Overcoming Emotional Chaos: Eliminate Anxiety, Lift Depression and Create Security in Your Life.* San Diego: Jodere Group, 2002.

15. Tiller WA, McCraty R, Atkinson M. Cardiac coherence: A new, noninvasive measure of autonomic nervous system order. *Alternative Therapies in Health and Medicine* 1996;2(1):52-65.

16. Pribram KH. Emotions: A neurobehavioral analysis. In: Scherer KR, Ekman P, eds. *Approaches to Emotion* Hillsdale, NJ: Erlbaum, 1984.

17. James W. What is an emotion? *Mind* 1884; 9(34): 188-205.

18. Ellsworth PC. William James and emotion: Is a century of fame worth a century of misunderstanding? *Psychological Review* 1994; 101(2):222-229.

19. Cannon WB. The James-Lange theory of emotion: A critical examination and an alternative theory. *American Journal of Psychology* 1927;39: 106-124.

20. Marshall LH, Magoun HW. *Discoveries in the Human Brain.* Totowa, NJ: Humana Press, 1998.

21. Cannon WB. *Bodily Changes in Pain, Hunger, Fear and Rage: An Account of Recent Researches into the Function of Emotional Excitement*, 2nd edition. New York: D. Appleton & Company, 1929.

22. Lindsley DB. Emotion. In: Stevens SS, ed. *Handbook of Experimental Psychology*. New York: Wiley, 1951: 473- 516.

23. Papez JW. A proposed mechanism of emotion. *Archives of Neurological Psychiatry* 1937;38: 725-743.

24. Hess WR. *Diencephalon: Autonomic and Extrapyramidal Functions.* New York: Grune & Stratton, 1954.

25. Lashley KS. The thalamus and emotion. In: Beach FA, Hebb DO, Morgan CT, Nissen HS, eds. *The Neurospsychology of Lashley.* New York: McGraw-Hill, 1960.

26. MacLean PD. Psychosomatic disease and the "visceral brain": Recent developments bearing on the Papez theory of emotion. *Psychosomatic Medicine* 1949; 11:338-353.

27. MacLean PD. Some psychiatric implications of physiological studies on frontotemporal portion of limbic system (visceral brain). *Electroencephalography and Clinical Neu- rophysiology* 1952;4:407-418.

28. MacLean PD. The triune brain, emotion and scientific bias. In: Schmitt FO, ed. *The Neurosciences: Second Study Program.* New York: Rockefeller University Press, 1970: 336-349

29. MacLean PD. *The Triune Brain in Evolution: Role in Paleocerebral Functions.*

New York: Plenum, 1990.

30. Butler AB, Hodos W. *Comparative Vertebrate Neuroanatomy: Evolution and Adaptation*. New York: Wiley-Liss, 1996

31. Flanigan S, Gabrieli ER, MacLean PD. Cerebral changes revealed by radioautography with S35-labeled I-methionine. *Archives of Neurological Psychiatry* 1957; 77:588-594.

32. Kaada BR, Pribram KH, Epstein JA. Respiratory and vascular responses in monkeys from temporal pole, insula, orbital surface and cingulate gyrus. *Journal of Neurophysiology* 1949;12:347-356.

33. Seung HS. Half a century of Hebb. *Nature Neuroscience* 2000; 3:1166.

34. Abbott LF, Nelson SB. Synaptic plasticity: Taming the beast. *Nature Neuroscience* 2000; 3:1178-1183.

35. Green E, quoted in CB Pert, *Molecules of Emotion* New York: Scribner, 1997, p. 137.

36. Schachter S, Singer JE. Cognitive, social, and physiological determinants of emotional state. *Psychological Review* 1962;69:379-399.

37. Gellhorn E, Loofbourrow GN. *Emotions and Emotional Disorders: A Neurophysiogical Study*. New York: Harper & Row, 1963.

38. Malmo RB, Shagass C, Davis FH. Symptom specificity and bodily reactions during psychiatric interview. Psychosomatic Medicine 1950; 12:362-376.

39. Ax AF. The physiological differentiation between fear and anger in humans. *Psychosomatic Medicine* 1953; 15: 433-442

40. Schachter J. Pain, fear, and anger in hypertensives and normotensives: A psychophysiological study. *Psychosomatic Medicine* 1957; 15:17-29.

41. Graham DT, Stern JA, Winokur G. Experimental investigation of the specificity of attitude hypothesis in psychosomatic disease. *Psychosomatic Medicine* 1958; 20:446-457.

42. Levenson RW, Ekman P, Friesen WV. Voluntary facial action generates emotion-specific autonomic nervous system activity. *Psychophysiology* 1990; 27:363-384.

43. Ekman P, Levenson RW, Friesen WV. Autonomic nervous system activity distinguishes among emotions. *Science* 1983; 221(4616):1208-1210.

44. Hubert W, de Jong-Meyer RD. Psychophysiological response patterns to positive and negative film stimuli. *Biological Psychology* 1991; 31(1):73-93.

45. Collet C, Vernet-Maury E, Delhomme G, Dittmar A. Autonomic nervous system response patterns specificity to basic emotions. *Journal of the Autonomic Nervous System* 1997; 62:45-57.

46. Sinha R, Lovallo WR, Parsons OA. Cardiovascular differentiation of emotions. *Psychosomatic Medicine* 1992; 54(4): 422-435.

47. Leek BF. Abdominal visceral receptors. In: Neil E, ed. *Handbook of Sensory Physiology*, Vol. 3. Heidelberg: Springer, 1972: 113-160.

48. Andrews PLR. Vagal afferent innervation of the gastrointestinal tract. *Progress in Brain Research* 1986; 67:65-86.
49. Neundörfer B, Hilz MJ. Ludwig Robert Müller (1870- 1962) – A pioneer of autonomic nervous system research. *Clinical Autonomic Research* 1998; 8:1-5.
50. Müller LR. Ueber die Beziehung von seelischen Empfindungen zu Herzstörungen. *Münchner Medizinische Wochenschrift* 1906; 53:14-16.
51. Heymans C, Neil E. *Reflexogenic Areas of the Cardiovascular System*. Boston: Little, Brown, 1958.
52. Lacey JI, Lacey BC. Some autonomic-central nervous system interrelationships. In: Black P, ed. *Physiological Correlates of Emotion*. New York: Academic Press, 1970: 205-227.
53. Bonvallet M, Allen MB. Prolonged spontaneous and evoked reticular activation following discrete bulbar lesions. *Electroencephalography and Clinical Neurophysiology* 1963; 15:969-988.
54. Gahery Y, Vigier D. Inhibitory effects in the cuneate nucleus produced by vago-aortic afferent fibers. *Brain Research* 1974; 75:241-246.
55. Randich A, Gebhart GF. Vagal afferent modulation of nociception. *Brain Research Reviews* 1992; 17:77-99.
56. Drinkhill MJ, Mary DA. The effect of stimulation of the atrial receptors on plasma cortisol level in the dog. *Journal of Physiology* 1989; 413:299-313.
57. Rau H, Pauli P, Brody S, Elbert T. Baroreceptor stimulation alters cortical activity. *Psychophysiology* 1993; 30: 322-325.
58. Sandman CA, Walker BB, Berka C. Influence of afferent cardiovascular feedback on behavior and the cortical evoked potential. In: Cacioppo JT, Petty RE, eds. *Perspectives in Cardiovascular Psychophysiology*. New York: The Guilford Press, 1982: 189-222.
59. van der Molen MW, Somsen RJM, Orlebeke JF. The rhythm of the heart beat in information processing. In: Ackles PK, Jennings JR, Coles MGH, eds. *Advances in Psychophysiology*, Vol. 1. London: JAI Press, 1985: 1-88.
60. Schandry R, Montoya P. Event-related brain potentials and the processing of cardiac activity. *Biological Psychology* 1996; 42:75-85.
61. Montoya P. *Herzwahrnehmung und hirnelektrische Aktivität. Eine Analyse der topographischen Verteilung von herzschlag-synchron evozierten Potentialen* (HEP). Frankfurt/Main: Peter Lang, 1994.
62. Rosenfeld SA. *Conversations between heart and brain* Rockville, MD: National Institute of Mental Health, 1978.
63. Lacey JI. Psychophysiological approaches to the evaluation of psychotherapeutic process and outcome. In: Rubinstein E, Parloff M, eds. *Research in Psychotherapy* Washington, DC: American Psychological Association, 1959: 160-208.
64. Lacey JI, Kagan J, Lacey BC, Moss HA. The visceral level: Situational determi-

nants and behavioral correlates of autonomic response patterns. In: Knapp PH, ed. *Expression of the Emotions in Man*. New York: International Universities Press, 1963: 161-196.

65. Lacey JI. Somatic response patterning and stress: Some revisions of activation theory. In: Appley MH, Trumbull R, eds. *Psychological Stress: Issues in Research*. New York: Appleton-Century-Crofts, 1967: 14-42.

66. Lacey BC, Lacey JI. Studies of heart rate and other bodily processes in sensorimotor behavior. In: Obrist PA, Black AH, Brener J, DiCara LV, eds. *Cardiovascular Psychophysiology: Current Issues in Response Mechanisms, Biofeedback, and Methodology*. Chicago: Aldine, 1974: 538-564.

67. Israel NR. Cognitive control and pattern of autonomic response. Paper presented at meeting of the Eastern Psychological Association, Washington, D.C., April, 1968.

68. Israel NR. Leveling-sharpening and anticipatory cardiac response. *Psychosomatic Medicine* 1969; 31:499-509.

69. Koriath JJ, Lindholm E. Cardiac-related cortical inhibition during a fixed foreperiod reaction time task. *International Journal of Psychophysiology* 1986; 4:183-195.

70. Walker BB, Sandman CA. Visual evoked potentials change as heart rate and carotid pressure change. *Psychophysiology* 1982; 19(5):520-527.

71. Schandry R, Sparrer B, Weitkunat R. From the heart to the brain: A study of heartbeat contingent scalp potentials. *International Journal of Neuroscience* 1986; 30:261-275.

72. Montoya P, Schandry R, Muller A. Heartbeat evoked potentials (HEP): Topography and influence of cardiac awareness and focus of attention. *Electroencephalography and Clinical Neurophysiology* 1993; 88:163-172.

73. Schandry R, Leopold C. The severity of diabetic autonomic neuropathy is reflected in the heartbeat evoked brain potential [abst.]. *Clinical Autonomic Research* 1997; 7(5): 249-250.

74. Lessmeier TJ, Gamperling D, Johnson-Liddon V, Fromm BS, Steinman RT, Meissner MD, Lehmann MH. Unrecognized paroxysmal supraventricular tachycardia: potential for mis-diagnosis as panic disorder. *Archives of Internal Medicine* 1997; 157:537-543.

75. McCraty R, Barrios-Choplin B, Rozman D, Atkinson M, Watkins AD. The impact of a new emotional self-management program on stress, emotions, heart rate variability, DHEA and cortisol. *Integrative Physiological and Behavioral Science* 1998; 33(2):151-170.

76. Aggleton JP, ed. *The Amygdala: Neurobiological Aspects of Emotion, Memory and Mental Dysfunction*. New York: Wiley-Liss, 1992.

77. Zhang JX, Harper RM, Frysinger RC. Respiratory modu- lation of neuronal discharge in the central nucleus of the amygdala during sleep and waking

states. *Experimental Neurology* 1986; 91:193-207.

78. Frysinger RC, Harper RM. Cardiac and respiratory correlations with unit discharge in epileptic human temporal lobe. *Epilepsia* 1990;31(2):162-171.

79. Pribram KH, Bagshaw MH. Further analysis of the tem- poral lobe syndrome utilizing fronto-temporal ablations. *Journal of Comparative Neurology* 1953; 99:347-375.

80. Pribram KH, Melges FT. Psychophysiological basis of emotion. In: Vinken PJ, Bruyn GW, eds. *Handbook of Clinical Neurology*. Amsterdam: North-Holland Publishing Company, 1969: 316-341.

81. James W. *Principles of Psychology*. New York: Holt, 1890

82. Näätänen R. *Attention and Brain Function*. Hillsdale, NJ: Lawrence Erlbaum Associates, 1992.

83. Sharpless S, Jasper H. Habituation of the arousal reaction. *Brain* 1956;79:655-680.

84. Miller GA, Galanter EH, Pribram KH. *Plans and the Structure of Behavior*. New York: Henry Holt & Co., 1960

85. Pribram KH. The new neurology and the biology of emotion: A structural approach. *American Psychologist* 1967; 22(10):830-838.

86. Pribram KH. *Languages of the Brain*. New York: Brandon House, 1971.

87. Armour JA. Peripheral autonomic neuronal interactions in cardiac regulation. In: Armour JA, Ardell JL, eds. *Neurocardiology*. New York: Oxford University Press, 1994: 219-244

88. Armour JA. *Neurocardiology—Anatomical and functional principles*. Boulder Creek: CA, HeartMath Research Center, Institute of HeartMath, Publication No. 03-011, 2003

89. Cantin M, Genest J. The heart as an endocrine gland. *Scientific American* 1986; 254(2):76-81.

90. Mukoyama M, Nakao K, Hosoda K, Suga S, Saito Y, Ogawa Y, Shirakami G, Jougasaki M, Obata K, Yasue H, et al. Brain natriuretic peptide as a novel cardiac hormone in humans. Evidence for an exquisite dual natriuretic peptide system, atrial natriuretic peptide and brain natriuretic peptide. *Journal of Clinical Investigation* 1991; 4:1402-1412.

91. Gutkowska J, Jankowski M, Mukaddam-Daher S, Mc-Cann SM. Oxytocin is a cardiovascular hormone. *Brazilian Journal of Medical and Biological Research* 2000; 33: 625-633.

92. Huang M-H, Friend DS, Sunday ME, Singh K, Haley K, Austen KF, Kelly RA, Smith TW. An intrinsic adrenergic system in mammalian heart. *Journal of Clinical Investiga- tion* 1996;98(6):1298-1303.

93. McCraty R, Atkinson M. *Psychophysiological coherence* Boulder Creek, CA: HeartMath Research Center, Institute of HeartMath, Publication 03-016, 2003.

94. Pribram KH. Feelings as monitors. In: Arnold MB, ed. *Feelings and Emotions.* New York: Academic Press, 1970: 41-53.

95. Pribram KH. Reinforcement revisited: A structural view. In Jones MR, ed. *Nebraska Symposium on Motivation* Lincoln: University of Nebraska Press, 1963: 113-159.

Rollin McCraty, Ph.D. is Director of Research of the HeartMath Research Center at the Institute of HeartMath. He is also an Adjunct Professor at Clemson University and Visiting Professor in the Department of Family and Community Medicine at the University of Alabama at Birmingham. A psychophysiologist, Dr. McCraty's research interests include the physiology of optimal function with a focus on the mechanisms by which emotions influence cognitive processes, behavior, and health as well as the global interconnectivity between people and the earth's energetic systems. Findings from this research have been applied to the development of tools and technology to optimize individual and organizational health, performance, and quality of life. He is a Fellow of the American Institute of Stress, holds memberships with the International Neurocardiology Network, American Autonomic Society, Pavlovian Society and Association for Applied Psychophysiology and Biofeedback among others. Dr. McCraty has acted as Principal Investigator in numerous laboratory research studies examining the effects of emotions on heart–brain interactions and on autonomic, cardiovascular, hormonal, and immune system function. He has also served as PI in a number of field studies to determine the outcomes of positive emotion-focused interventions and heart rhythm feedback in diverse organizational and educational settings as well as in various clinical populations. Dr. McCraty and his research team regularly participate in collaborative studies with other U.S. and international scientific, medical and educational institutions; they have worked in partnership with research groups at Stanford University, Wake Forest University, the US Navy and Air Force, Miami Heart Research Institute, and Claremont Graduate University among many others. His research has been published in journals that include the American Journal of Cardiology, Journal of the American College of Cardiology, Stress Medicine, Biological Psychology and Integrative Physiological and Behavioral Science.

The Unexpected Interdependence of Heart and Mind

Haley Peckham

The nature of the relationship between our hearts and minds, our passion and our reason, has occupied us for centuries. In the 17th century, the theologian Jacques-Bénigne Bossuet captured the essence of the heart's wisdom and mystery when he stated, "The heart has reasons which reason does not know". In the following century, the British philosopher David Hume claimed, "Reason is, and ought only to be the slave of the passions", and a hundred years later we find Van Gogh entreating his brother to not forget "… that the little emotions are the great captains of our lives, and we obey them without knowing it". These quotes privilege emotion and passion as our driving force and suggest that our heart, the place of our truest feelings, cannot really be known or understood by our mind—or, were it possible, that it may not even be desirable. Perhaps influenced by Freud's topographical model where the rampant base appetites and instinctual drives of the *id* had to be kept in check by the idealistic, guiding, and often harsh *superego*, and a perhaps somewhat harassed negotiator, the *ego*, the tide turned from privileging emotion to privileging reason—using our so-called "superior" intellect and our morality to keep our unruly (even dangerous) emotions, passions, and urges under control, in order to become civilised, to be a good and sensible person. Perhaps, however, we all intuitively know and feel that these two most precious organs—the heart and the mind—have some kind of relationship, and perhaps too we sense a battle for dominance, listening to our head or our heart, yet at some other times or contexts, having identified shared goals, our head and heart work in harmony to achieve them. Contemporary physiological and neuroscientific research suggests that the relationship between our rationality and our emotionality—our hearts and our minds—is interdependent, adaptive, and exquisitely complex. Now, intriguingly, it has been established that measures of our heart rate variability are extraordinarily well correlated with our capacity for emotional self-regulation and social engagement, and this fascinating observation is the subject of this article.

A contemporary view on emotion put forward by Leslie Greenberg, one of the original developers of emotion-focused therapy, is that emotions communicate to us what is significant for our wellbeing. Essentially, when we are open to our emotions, we can hear what they are saying and respond meaningfully. In

111

just the same way that we open the fridge when we're hungry, or head straight for the vending machine when we're absolutely starving, our feelings are telling us something about ourselves—about how we're doing—that needs to be felt, heard, and responded to appropriately. This seems very obvious in the example of hunger; but even subtle and complex feelings—feeling slighted, satisfied, disappointed, ambivalent, irritated, guilty, jealous, enraged—are all pieces of information that convey a message about our wellbeing and tell us how we are doing in a particular situation or context, or with a particular person or group of people in our world. This view of the emotions is consistent with an evolutionary perspective. Greenberg writes that emotions are a "fundamentally adaptive resource" and that the information provided by our feelings helps us to evaluate our unique experience of the world and take action to get our needs met, our desires fulfilled, and a step nearer to achieving our goals. In this way emotions assist us to adapt to our world to promote survival and help us thrive. Likewise, our capacity for reason can draw on our emotionally felt experiences to make decisions that also serve us. This view is reflected by the neurobiologist, Antonio Damasio, in his book *Descartes' Error: Emotion, reason and the human brain*, which is predicated on the idea that far from emotions being "intruders on the bastion of reason", the capacity to attend to and feel one's emotions may underlie the ability to reason effectively.

Although being able to think and reason effectively about anything of importance to us can require us to reflect on and think about our emotions, we can also be moved to act on the basis of our emotions without thought or reason. Emotions are often written about as originating from bottom up or top down processing or, in Joseph LeDoux's terms, being generated by the low road or the high road. What these terms refer to is the flexible capacity of our brains to respond to a situation with either an immediate, urgent emotional experience and an absolute imperative to act, such as in the case of fear or rage, which is the low road or bottom up processing; or to reflect on a situation or circumstance, generating an experience of emotion that is integrated with thought, perhaps leading to a considered action, which is the top down or the high road of emotion. What bottom up or low road processing buys us in evolutionary terms is, as you would expect, related to our survival. A fast and dirty bottom up appraisal of a situation, which generates fear and makes us scream and run or fight for our lives, serves our survival in a threat context far better than a slow, considered, emotional and thoughtful response. In threat circumstances it is the paranoid rabbit that survives, not the more laid back and thoughtful bunny. LeDoux illustrates this with the example of seeing what looks like a snake in front of you. Clearly, in this situation, it is far better to take evasive action and subsequently realise it was stick than to not take evasive action until you are sure it is a snake, during which time you could have been bitten. Hence our emotional responses serve our survival. In non-threatening situations our emotions can be felt, reflected on and thought about before any action need be taken, but in threat situations, where we don't feel safe, reflection and thought are expendable, and the fast and dirty emotional appraisal that promotes safety and survival dominates. For those of us who have experienced trauma, our feeling of safety is fragile and easily perturbed, and we may be hypervigilant to threat cues. In our case, our brain has adapted to the experience of not "being" safe by not "anticipating" safe—and that may mean we are less able to keep our reflective appraisal on line, which would help us to thoughtfully respond, and instead we are set up to react with our fast and dirty emotional appraisal that tells us we are not safe and we have to DO something. Unfortunately our evolutionarily sculpted, survival-serving, default—that is, to interpret ambiguous information as threatening—may mean that our tendency to react emotionally, rather than respond emotionally and thoughtfully, causes problems for us in relationships or at work.

The lack of an ability to reflect on our emotions, or emotionally self-regulate, leaves us unhelpfully stuck with our low road, bottom up experience of emotions. A capacity to regulate our emotions involves top down or high road processing—and enough of a sense of safety—to be able to employ these strategies. To a great extent, this capacity for effective emotional self-regulation is an outcome of how effectively our caregivers were able to regulate their own emotions, and ours, when we were infants and children. Relational trauma, abuse, neglect, and hostile or invalidating caregiver responses are all experiences that compromise a child's sense of safety and capacity to develop effective top down emotional self-regulation. Theorists and researchers have discovered that heart rate variability is a reliable marker of an individual's capacity for emotional self-regulation and social engagement—but how can a measure of variability between heartbeats index something as sophisticated and subtle as our ability to emotionally self-regulate and socially engage?

Heart rate variability is, as it sounds, the degree of variability of the time between heartbeats and is essentially a readout of the extent to which the heart is under parasympathetic influence. Recall from biology that our autonomic nervous system is divided into sympathetic (fight and flight) and parasympathetic (rest and digest) influences. The parasympathetic innervation via the vagus nerve of the heart's intrinsic pacemaker (the sino-atrial node) puts a vagal brake on the heart, inhibiting it from yammering away at 100 beats per minute to the more steadfast and normal 70 beats per minute, which is average for adults. What this means is that our normal resting heart rate is an outcome of our pacemaking sino-atrial node being opposed and slowed down by our parasympathetic vagus nerve. To achieve an increase in heart rate it is sufficient that the default parasympathetic inhibition is itself inhibited without any requirement of sympathetic heart rate activation. Additionally, any variation in the degree of parasympathetic inhibition will swiftly affect heart rate, but sympathetic influence is slower. What this essentially boils down to is that a heart with a high heart rate variability is a heart that is highly influenced by the vagal brake of the parasympathetic nervous system. So how does our parasympathetic vagus nerve link heart rate variability to emotional self-regulation and social engagement?

The vagus nerve is a channel of communication between the brain and the body. It carries afferent information about the body (in this case the heart) to the brain, and it also carries efferent information from the brain to the heart. This integrating nerve is the crucial link in the brain-heart connection. The brain structures involved in both receiving information about, and sending information to, the heart are collectively called the Central Autonomic Network and include the anterior cingulate, the amygdala, the prefrontal cortices, the hypothalamus, the nucleus of the solitary tract, and regions of the medulla. The prefrontal cortices, in particular, are involved in self-regulatory functions—such as the ability to reflect and plan and how to behave socially. In situations perceived by the individual as non-threatening, the prefrontal cortex inhibits sympathetic circuits in lower (i.e., evolutionarily older) brain regions, including the amygdala. The prefrontal cortex is where top down or high road emotional processing originates, and the influence of the prefrontal cortex via the parasympathetic vagus nerve is what makes heart rate variability an index of emotional self-regulation and social engagement.

It is important to recognise that the prefrontal cortex is a unique region of the brain; and although it has evolved in all of us, it is more or less well developed in individuals. The prefrontal cortex is highly adaptive and experience dependent: the actual life we have lived is etched into the architecture of this exquisitely adaptive brain region. Hence the development of our prefrontal cortex is in large part an outcome of the kinds of care we received as infants—how much our caregivers were able to recognise our emotions, and give names to them, and engage with us in soothing and regulating those emotions to help us feel reassured and safe again. If we had poor care, or experienced emotional neglect, abuse, or relational trauma, we have not been helped to feel safe and our prefrontal cortex is impoverished as a result; it has simply not had the opportunity or the types of experiences needed for it to develop so that it can inhibit our sympathetically driven, survival-geared, threat-sensitive, evolutionarily older, brain regions. A less well-developed prefrontal cortex cannot efficiently inhibit sympathetic survival-geared, threat-sensing neural networks, so there is simply less parasympathetic vagal activity arriving at our heart, culminating in a low heart rate variability.

If we have haven't had the kinds of experiences that develop our prefrontal cortex and capacity for emotional self-regulation, engaging in psychotherapy is a way we can choose to address this—though it is doubtful that someone will arrive at your rooms requesting that you help "develop their prefrontal cortex and top down emotional regulation". The process of psychotherapy helps us feel, recognise, express, soothe, and reflect on our emotions—all of which will increase the capacity of our prefrontal cortex to engage in the top down, high road processing of emotions that facilitates our being responsive and able to respond, rather than just being emotionally reactive in situations. Another way of saying the same thing is that psychotherapy helps to develop our prefrontal cortex so that lower brain region sympathetic activity can be inhibited, and the prefrontal cortex can literally send a message to the threat-sensing regions saying, "Hey, it's ok! It's safe enough—there is time and space to feel and think here. No need to react just yet!" This message of safety is a parasympathetic message, conveyed via the vagal nerve to the heart, and it will increase heart rate variability.

The polyvagal theory (so named because there is a mammalian and a reptilian part of the vagus nerve) formalises the heart-mind connection as neural circuits, which (although interconnected) are evolutionarily distinct and support different adaptive strategies for survival, such as social bonding, or the fight or flight or feigning death responses. Stephen Porges, the author of the theory, suggests there are three circuits that promote adaptive survival in different circumstances, namely safety, danger, and extreme threat to life. The parasympathetic vagus nerve detailed above—which is more accurately termed the mammalian, myelinated vagus nerve—connects the central autonomic neural network to the heart. It is the most recently evolved adaptive strategy, which serves both survival and procreation by promoting bonding and facilitating emotional self-regulation and social engagement in circumstances of safety. This myelinated vagal brake increases heart rate variability and a related measure—respiratory sinus arrhythmia—and it also affects the muscles of the face to enable engaging facial expressions and thereby promote social adaption. The sympathetic nervous system is more defensive, supporting fight or flight behaviours in dangerous circumstances; but in life-threatening circumstances an extreme and primitive parasympathetic adaption, acting through the reptilian, unmyelinated portion of the vagus nerve, takes over, allowing an organism to feign death by producing *neurogenic bradycardia*, literally a slow heart rate induced by a nervous response. All three systems have survival value and are adaptive for differing circumstances of threat, ranging from extreme threat to life to no threat (i.e., safety), where there is opportunity to form social bonds. Threat is perceived through what Porges terms *neuroception*, meaning the continuous feedback that subcortical regions receive about the environment and the state of the body. In response to this information the most adaptive circuit is selected for the perceived circumstance. The perception of threat is thus linked to the mammalian parasympathetic vagal brake going off line—and with it the capacity for emotional self-regulation and social engagement—and instead defaulting to the next best adaption, a sympathetically driven fight or flight defensive response.

The perception of threat is a key issue because, although our brains have commonly evolved structures to support a top down or high road capacity for emotional regulation, our brains may not have had the types of experiences that allow us to develop that capacity. As described above, if we grew up feeling mostly safe and protected, and our caregivers were able to modulate their own emotional responses and provide sensitive, affective attunement to us as infants and children, then in all likelihood we will have developed the capacity for top down or high road emotional processing and be able to utilise our myelinated parasympathetic vagus nerve to help us regulate ourselves and maintain a high heart rate variability. Even in ambiguous or difficult circumstances we may be able to keep our thinking and feeling, highly evolved mammalian brain on line and not default into fight or flight, sympathetic threat-driven responses. If, on the other hand, we have not been fortunate enough to grow up feeling safe and protected, with emotionally literate, reflective, loving caregivers and have instead felt frightened or been exposed to threat in the form of neglect, abuse, or caregiver hostility, we will not have had the opportunity to develop the emotional regulation and social engagement that our mammalian brain affords us—we haven't been safe enough—hence we very easily feel threatened and very readily default into bottom up or low road processing with its fast and dirty emotional appraisal and defensive, sympathetic fight or flight behaviours.

Research into Borderline Personality Disorder (BPD) is consistent with a polyvagal understanding. BPD is characterised by emotional instability, persistent fear of abandonment, suicidal thoughts, lack of capacity for emotional regulation, and marked instability in relationships. The histories and narratives of sufferers of BPD are infused with stories of neglect, relational trauma, emotional, physical, or sexual abuse, caregiver hostility, and immense loss—exactly the kinds of experiences that deny a child the opportunity to develop the potential of their mammalian brain and become able to emotionally self-regulate or reflect or engage positively and socially. Such children have simply not had the kinds of experiences that could allow them to develop these capacities. Recent research has suggested that people with BPD would not have developed the capacity for robust parasympathetic vagal influence over their heart rate variability and would thus have a pronounced tendency to default to a sympathetic influence in social contexts. People with BPD are traumatised; they suffer from the capacity that all brains demonstrate—that is, the capacity to adapt. Rather, their brains have adapted to threat because they have learnt through traumatic or life-threatening experience to anticipate traumatic and life threatening experiences; they have learnt that they are not safe, and that the world is not safe. Consequently, it is impossible for them to hold on to the insufficient scraps of emotional self-regulation that they can muster because their hypersensitised perception of threat constantly triggers them into sympathetic dominance and drives the fight or flight behaviours that shape the characteristic emotional and relational instability of this disorder.

Darwin's perspective was that an organism's capacity to adapt to its particular environment was the ultimate deciding factor on whether that species would survive. The interconnectedness of heart and mind through the vagal nerve, formalised by the polyvagal theory, exemplifies the sophisticated and elegant adaptations made over the whole course of our evolution. From this evolutionary perspective we can see ancient survival strategies still in place for times of terror and threat to life, where the evolutionarily ancient, unmyelinated, reptilian vagus nerve makes us freeze and feign death. More recent evolution has seen the development of our myelinated, mammalian vagus nerve and prefrontal cortex, which facilitate our capacity to reflect on emotions and social situations and thus choose how we behave and respond in them. Intrinsic to these different adaptions is our neuroceptive ability, the unconscious monitoring of threat in the environment. It is our perception of threat that really chooses our strategy for us. Less threat and more feeling safe allows us to use our reflective capacities, our high road top down processing. Less safety and more threat means we cannot keep our reflective feeling and thinking capacities on line and instead default into defensive fight or flight sympathetic strategies. Although evolution has helpfully provided us with an unmyelinated vagus nerve and a pre frontal cortex, it is our unique experiences of threat, safety, emotional regulation, and soothing that sculpt our prefrontal cortex and determine its capacity to provide that top down regulation—the ability to respond rather than react—and, at a biological level, the ability to inhibit sympathetic fight or flight responses. Our capacity to use our prefrontal cortex, to reflect, to respond thoughtfully, and not to trigger into fight or flight behaviours, is not an act of will, nor is it something we are able to choose or can be held accountable for. It is an indicator of how threatened we feel and also how threatened we have habitually felt throughout our lives.

This is not something we should be judged for—but neither is it immutable. Our habitual feelings of threat, and our fast and dirty emotional appraisals, which frequently take us into highly emotional and usually very painful conflicts with people close to us, can be changed. We need the kinds of experiences that will help us develop the frontal cortex. We need experiences that—although they will be emotionally provocative—will stay safe enough that we can feel and think. We need someone steadfast who can help to soothe us and untangle, if the threat we feel now is the anticipation of threat (because we have never been safe), or if it is actually safe enough now to feel and think. We need a new emotional, thoughtful experience that is safe enough. Whilst we cannot choose how safe we feel from moment to moment, we can make a "bigger picture" choice to address how the lack of safety in our past is shaping our anticipation of threat now. We can choose new experiences that will help us feel habitually safer and allow us more room to choose and respond. We can choose to change our heart and mind connection—and one way to do this might be psychotherapy.

Haley Peckham has a degree in philosophy, and Masters degrees in Philosophy of Cognitive Science and Molecular Neuroscience. Following training and working as a mental health nurse in the UK she is now studying for a PhD in Neuroscience at the Uni of Melbourne and training to be a psychotherapist.

HEARTMATH
INTERVIEW WITH ROLLIN McCRATY, PhD

David Van Nuys

Introduction: My guest today is Dr. Rollin McCraty, and we'll be discussing the benefits of heart coherence and other matters of the heart. Rollin McCraty, PhD has worked in the Institute of HeartMath since its inception in 1991. Working with the institute founder, Doc Childre, Dr. McCraty developed the organization's research goals and created the institute's scientific advisory board.

McCraty is a Fellow of the American Institute of Stress, holds memberships with the International Neurocardiology Network, American Autonomic Society, Pavlovian Society and Association for Applied Psychophysiology and Biofeedback, and is an adjunct professor at Claremont Graduate University.

Dr. McCraty and his team regularly participate in collaborative studies with other U.S. and international scientific, medical and educational institutions. They have worked in partnership with research groups at Stanford University, Dalhousie University in Halifax, Nova Scotia, and the Miami Heart Research Institute, among many others.

Dr. McCraty has authored dozens of research studies, many of which have been published in peer-reviewed journals including the American Journal of Cardiology, the Journal of the American College of Cardiology, Stress Medicine, Biological Psychology, and Integrative Physiological and Behavioral Science. In 2010, Alternative Therapies in Health and Medicine, a respected peer-reviewed journal, dedicated an entire issue to the topic of coherence. Dr. McCraty wrote the lead article for this issue. Many of the other research studies represented in this issue examined the implications of HeartMath techniques and technology in a variety of settings and applications.

You can obtain a free e-book on HeartMath at http://www.heartmath.org/free-ebook-emotional-stress. Now, here is the interview.

Dr. Dave: Dr. Rollin McCraty, welcome to Shrink Rap Radio.

Dr. McCraty: Well thank you, good day.

Dr. Dave: It's great to have you on the show. I don't know if you'll recognize the name of my good friend, Dr. Dale Ironson, who for years has been singing the praises of HeartMath to me. Does that name ring a bell for you?

Dr. McCraty: It does, yes. In fact if I have it right, I think we were at a board meeting together in the UK a few years ago. That's how I first met her.

Dr. Dave: No, you are thinking of his sister, Dr. Gale Ironson. I'm talking about the brother, Dr. Dale Ironson.

Dr. McCraty: Oh right, right—yes, yes, you are absolutely right. I misheard you. It does ring a bell, yes.

Dr. Dave: He's been a good friend for a long time, and I've also interviewed the pair of them on the show a long time back. And then more recently I seem to be hearing about HeartMath in other places, and I even had a recent listener request to do a show on it. So I'm really glad to have you here to fill us in on HeartMath.

Dr. McCraty: My pleasure.

Dr. Dave: So I think the place for us to start is for me to ask you, just what is HeartMath?

Dr. McCraty: That is always a hard question to answer because it's so many things in different ways. We're a research-based organization. Basically Heart-Math is a system of tools, techniques and technologies that allows people to bring their physical, mental and emotional systems into balance and alignment. And I'm going to add, with their heart's intuitive guidance, to help them unfold through the process of becoming who they really are at a deeper level: heart-empowered beings.

Dr. Dave: You know, it strikes me for the first time right now that the word HeartMath is almost an oxymoron. It might seem that way because we don't tend to associate the heart with mathematics. So how is it that you arrived at that name?

Dr. McCraty: OK, well that's an interesting story too. "HeartMath" was coined by the founder of HeartMath, Doc Childre, and what he really meant by that name was to put the heart, which is usually thought of as a kind of a mushy or Valentine's day thing, together with the intelligence of the heart which is what we are talking about.

That's one answer to it. And another is that through our inner heart's guidance there are psychological formulas, if you will, where if we do X we will get Y result. So that's another aspect of where the name came from.

Dr. Dave: To what extent are we talking about the physical heart as opposed to the metaphorical heart—and maybe there's a relationship between the two?

Dr. McCraty: Well absolutely, and we are talking about both. I mean obviously we do a lot of work with the physical heart and that's where a lot of our publications are based, in cardiology and biological psychiatry. All these kinds of publications have to do with our work on measuring the heart's rhythm or heart rate variability. And I think we are probably best known for being the original people who discovered that our current emotional state is reflected in the rhythmic patterns of the heartbeats, kind of like Morse code. We are probably about 80–85% accurate in detecting someone's emotional state just by looking at the pattern of their heart rhythm, whether they are conscious of the emotion or not. The body doesn't lie, and the heart really tells us what's going on. So that's on the physical side. Then there's the anatomy of heart-brain communication, which is all really important stuff.

We are also investigating what you would call the spiritual heart, or energetic heart. I don't think it's metaphorical so much. Some of our evidence is starting to say that there really is an energetic system. By energetic system I am talking about things we can't put under a microscope. You can't see a feeling or a thought. You know, it's not a physical thing that you can put an electrode in or, like I said, put under a microscope. So that's what I mean by energetic system, taking the mystery out of it.

For example, some of our work on what I like to call the electro-physiology of intuition shows that the heart is actually the first system of the body to respond to a future unknown stimulus. It then literally sends a measurably different neurological signal to the brain, informing it, and the body then responds. We call that the gut feeling, or the intuition. So I think that is some of the best evidence yet that the great writers of the past have been right all along when they talk about the heart being the window or the primary channel, if you will, to wisdom, to a higher capacity, our higher self. Every culture has its own word for that part of ourselves, for our "undivided wholeness", if we use a physics way of saying it.

Dr. Dave: Wow, you've really opened up a whole lot of possible directions here, and I'm particularly interested in this intuitive anticipation that you mention which almost sounds like what in the past would have been called ESP or precognition. Would I be right about that?

Dr. McCraty: Well yeah, and some of my colleagues have done work and have called it precognition. And now they have pretty much stopped using that term, because cognition is not involved. We always want to give the higher brain responsibility for everything, and it's just not the case always. I think intuition is a much better term. Now when we talk about "intuition"—just to help the listeners to understand where I am coming from here, because that term gets used a lot and for different things embraced under it—from our research we see that there are three different types of intuition.

Now, most of the academic writings on this topic are really to do with what is called implicit knowledge or implicit learning. And of course that's a very real and very important aspect of intuition. Basically it means that we learn something that we didn't know we had learned and that we forgot we learned. Then when we are faced with a new problem that we have no solution for, we are chewing on it a little bit. And we are either driving to work or not thinking about it or we're in the shower or something like that and —voilà—the answer seeps up from our unconscious to our conscious and we have the insight. That's certainly an aspect of intuition.

The second type of intuition is what we call energetic sensitivity. That's where our nervous systems are actually sensitive to other very real, measurable signals in the environment. For example, most people might have had the experience of feeling like somebody is staring at you and you turn around and, sure enough, there *is* someone staring at you.

Dr. Dave: Yeah, boy, I've certainly had that experience.

Dr. McCraty: Another example of energetic sensitivity is that some people have sensitivity to earthquakes. They can feel them coming. And we now know that you can measure changes in the earth's magnetic fields prior to an earthquake. Animals are also great examples, they are very tuned in and there are lots and lots of examples of this.

Some people have more sensitivity for these kinds of things. Empathy would be another thing in this category where we are reading different kinds of signals, especially ones that our heart and body are radiating. These examples are all in the energetic sensitivity category. We've done a lot of work here in our lab to verify this, to kind of take the mystery out of it and make it very rigorous science.

And the third type of intuition we call non-local. One example that a lot of people can relate to is when you are driving down a road that you've gone down many, many times before, and for some reason that you might not even be conscious of, you slow down before you go around a curve or over a hill, and sure enough, there is either a police car or a child running out onto the street or an accident or something that would have probably caused a problem if you had not slowed down. Most people have actually had that experience. Or you are thinking about somebody and the phone rings and it's them, that kind of thing. Those are examples that you cannot really explain through implicit learning or implicit knowledge.

There are some very rigorous studies now, not only ones conducted here in our facility but by a few other people also, that have all kind of confirmed that intuition is a real and a measurable thing. What we're also finding as we get what we call more "heart coherent", which is a physiological measure of the alignment of our inner systems and also the alignment between our mind, emotions and body, is that we have more access to all those types of intuition. So we are really able to access more of that kind of information in our day-to-day lives.

Dr. Dave: Well, thank you for breaking that down for us. And I'll let you know right up front that I am not a skeptic when it comes to the kind of experiences you are describing. So you don't have to worry about having to defend yourself.

Dr. McCraty: OK, that's nice to know. Some people are, you know, "Don't confuse me with the data, my mind is already made up"— you know.

Dr. Dave: Yeah, I know.

Dr. McCraty: I'm glad to hear you are not one of those.

Dr. Dave: Yeah. At the same time, I know your title there is Director of Research and I'm sure listeners would be interested to know, what is your training and background in terms of scientific research?

Dr. McCraty: Oh sure. My first life, as I like to call it, was in electrical engineering, and I worked for Motorola for a while as a systems engineer going out and solving problems people couldn't solve in the field. Then I started my own company, which was a research and development company in the field of electrostatics. And we became a pretty successful company inventing new technologies and so on. The short story here is that I basically made a lot of money doing that and got to a place in my own life where saving the life of another microprocessor wasn't really that fulfilling or having another sports car in the driveway wasn't going to do it for me .

That's when I met Doc Childre and got back more into my humanity side of things, and I really wanted to do something that made a difference. I understood what he was talking about in terms of the heart and it not just being a metaphor for a more intelligent type of system. It got me intrigued, and I tried it in my own life—some of what he was talking about. This was long before there was HeartMath Institute. And it worked for me. I had more personal gains in a three-month period after really giving it a serious try than I'd had in fifteen years of meditative-type practices. Then I basically became a psycho-physiologist and got a Ph.D. in psycho-physiology—ten, twelve years ago, whatever it was—to do the kind of research we do here. So all of my background in electrical engineering and all that was perfect for what I do now.

Dr. Dave: Wow, that's really fascinating. I had originally planned to be an electrical engineer myself, but my path deviated from that. What was the practice that Doc Childre engaged you in when you say you tried meditation but it wasn't really working for you? Evidently he introduced you to a practice that was fairly dramatic for you.

Dr. McCraty: I won't say meditation didn't work for me for me. It did. During those years I took a company from a startup in a garage to a fifteen million dollar company, so I had a great time through all that. Don't get me wrong, it was a fun ride. So I was serious about meditation, but I never really got stuck into the new-age kind of stuff at the same time. So I'm not saying it didn't help, that it wasn't helpful.

What Doc Childre introduced me to was the idea of the...even in the meditation practices—I'll back up here—a lot of talk goes on about the heart, about how you need to come from your heart and listen to your heart, all that, but it's still really more head-driven, mind-driven.

Dr. Dave: OK.

Dr. McCraty: You know, you whip your energy through your chakras and this and that and through the heart. And what Doc Childre was talking about was the heart, the energetic and spiritual heart, being a very real part of our nature and that it operated in what you could think of as another dimension of intelligence.

And so it was about really going into the heart and letting it run the show to access that other level of our inner intelligence. At that time this involved focusing one's energy in the heart center and accessing that deeper intelligence. And a lot of it had to do at that time, and it still does, really, with activating a sense of appreciation or deeper care.

This helps bring our systems into alignment to access the deeper part of ourselves. So I just simply tried that. We now call it "heart-focused breathing", to put your attention in the heart and breath as though you are breathing in and out of the heart area. I was really becoming more aware of my inner systems and was especially appreciating life and people. So it's what really made the difference for me: accessing that intelligence, that deeper intelligence.

It's really hard to talk about this stuff because so much of it is a personal kind of experience—people have to have it to get it.

Dr. Dave: Well, as difficult as it may be to talk about, I really appreciate you sharing your experience with it. Now a lot of my listeners are either therapists or are on their way to becoming therapists. Do you see HeartMath as a form of psychotherapy, or do you see it more as a human potential tool? You know, where would you place it?

Dr. McCraty: Well I wouldn't necessarily put it the psychotherapy category, but it's certainly a set of tools and techniques for expanding human potential. As I said earlier, it is helping people become who they really are at that deeper, inner core level. So HeartMath tools and techniques are certainly used in many therapy modalities now. I think last I heard, over thirty MBA hospitals and military hospitals are actively using HeartMath for a wide range of things: everything from pain management to helping with reintegration, PTSD, traumatic brain injury—just on that side of things.

HeartMath is used widely in alcohol and drug rehabilitation centers. What HeartMath is, if I can say it in another way, is tools and techniques to help us self-regulate but from a more intelligent, inner reference place or point. That's really what it's about from my perspective.

When we look at most of the problems we face either clinically or in society, it gets down to a lack of being able to be in charge of ourselves, to self-regulate. So ultimately HeartMath is giving you very practical, intentionally simple tools to do that, to self- regulate, to manage your emotions and behaviors.

Dr. Dave: Yeah, and given some of the applications that you mentioned, it seems like it would, at the very least, be a good tool for a therapist to have in their toolbox.

Dr. McCraty: Oh absolutely, yes. In fact we have a certification program just for healthcare professionals. A lot of healthcare professionals, including psychotherapists, social workers, but also cardiologists and people treating physical diseases have gone through that course. Basically when you use these techniques there's a measureable physiological change that goes along with them. Of course this centers on the activity of the heart. So again a lot of our work, on the science side, has been to study the physiology of all of what we call the coherent state.

A lot of people don't realize that the heart sends more information neurologically to the brain than the other way around. I can't take credit for that. This been known since the late 1800s, just largely forgotten and ignored. Yet those signals that the heart sends to our brain have profound effects on brain function, on our emotional experiences and our cognitive abilities. What a lot of therapists in many different disciplines have found is that if they get their client into a coherent state before they do whatever their choice of therapy is, they have much better outcomes, because they are getting people stabilized.

Coherence is a more stable state from a physiological perspective. It stabilizes the emotions and it facilitates mental functions. So whatever it is you are trying to do, you typically have better outcomes if you are in a more coherent state before you engage in it. Hopefully that makes sense the way I said it.

Dr. Dave: You may be speaking to what was to be my next question, which is, what sort of scientific validation is available for HeartMath's claims? I don't know if you've made any claims yet. I guess you have about self-regulation, emotional balance and so on. So what more can you tell us about the scientific validation?

Dr. McCraty: Probably the easiest place for people to go would be the Institute of HeartMath website, which is heartmath.org. On the website there is a section called Research Publications and there are many, many publications there. There are clinical studies on everything from blood pressure reduction to congestive heart failure, to reduced depression and anxiety, improved test scores, group cognitive function studies, PTSD, and brain injury. There's everything that I mentioned earlier and a lot of the basic research understanding the physiology of coherence—heart-rate and communications studies—which have been published here, because we are basically a research facility. But most of the clinical outcome studies have all been independent studies done by either medical institutions or all kinds of independent partners.

A lot of our work has been verified now independently and published by a large number of different institutions and researchers. So again there are some overview papers which might be a good place to start. You'll find a lot of publications. There's not only one or two. It's a pretty long list.

Dr. Dave: That's great to know. People who want to find out more will be able to do that.

That's wonderful. You've mentioned several times the term "coherence", the "heart's coherence", and I'm wondering both from a subjective point of view and an objective point of view, what does heart coherence look like? How does one know either subjectively and/or objectively when they are in that state?

Dr. McCraty: Well let's talk of the objectively first.

Dr. Dave: OK.

Dr. McCraty: I think that's the more important thing. In fact, since we have discovered the coherent state, our sister company HeartMath LLC has come out with simple little inexpensive devices to actually measure coherence physiologically.

Dr. Dave: I was wondering if you had something like that.

Dr. McCraty: The way coherence is assessed at a physiological level is looking at what's called heart-rate variability. That's probably a term that will be familiar to some listeners because it has become so popular in recent years. For those who aren't familiar with that term, in a healthy person, a resilient individual, our heart rate varies with each and every heartbeat. And that's called heart rate variability, which is very different from just heart rate, which is simply how many times the heart beats in a minute. So our heart is actually varying with each and every heartbeat. That's going on all the time even if we are asleep or resting or whatever.

As for the amount of this intrinsic natural variability, we have a lot more of it when we are young. We have less as we age. Now measuring how much variability we have we can pretty much tell, within an accuracy of two years, how old someone is. There is a very strong relationship between age and the amount of variability. So if we are depleting ourselves with stress, and it's usually psychological stress, anxiety, anger and irritation—these kinds of things that deplete our psycho-physiological system—this shows up in reduced variability or reduced resilience. That's one level of variability.

Now there's another, deeper level of looking at variability, which is, what's the pattern? You can think of this loosely as the heart beating out a message, kind of like Morse code, and that's what's reflecting our current emotional state and, to some degree, our mental state. This is where a picture is worth a thousand words. When we are in a state of anger or frustration, anxiety, fear, and so on, our heart rhythm becomes a very chaotic-looking pattern. We now know that you can actually do discrete emotion detection just from this pattern.

When we are in a positive state, when we are really feeling good and feeling a sense of adventure, enjoying life and having feelings of appreciation, compassion and care, the heart beats out a very different message, a very different pattern that's like sine waves, rolling hills.

This is ultimately reflected in our nervous system, our autonomic nervous system. So on the negative side of things, when we are frustrated and so on, the activity between the two branches of the autonomic nervous system, the sympathetic and parasympathetic, is literally out of sync. It's a lot like trying to drive your car with one foot on the accelerator and the other foot on the brake at the same time. It's a really good analogy, because most people get that "Oh, we shouldn't do that, it's no good for the car, we'll wear out the brakes faster and use more gas to get where we're going, and it's kind of a jerky ride." It's a great analogy, because these are all the same things that are going on inside of our body.

Now, because of the fact that the heart sends more information to the brain neurologically speaking than the other way around, there are very strong neural connections from the afferent or ascending pathways of the heart to key brain centers which are involved in a lot of different things like emotional experience.

Another one's the thalamus. The thalamus ultimately synchronizes the electrical activity of all the neurons in our brain. So when we have those erratic heart rhythms, which are associated with anger and so on, they basically interfere with the thalamus's ability to synchronize cortical activity...not that you have ever done this...where people might get a little angry with someone and say or do something out of anger that they regret a minute later; and I remember myself having done this once—I'm joking of course—thinking, "Where was my brain? I can't believe I just said that!"

Dr. Dave: Yeah.

Dr. McCraty: That's the physiology of it, kind of simply said. However, when we are in a coherent state, the electrical activity in the nervous system is synchronized—literally in sync—and you literally have a very harmonious inner rhythm going on. This is what's associated with positive feelings.

So this can quite easily be objectively measured, and very inexpensively. We use this widely now in many healthcare settings to help train individuals about how to get into this coherent state, this optimal state that's associated with the things we talked about earlier: emotional stability, improved cognitive and mental function, improved memory, blood pressure reduction, and so on.

It's a great training tool, but the thing to really emphasize is that it's there to facilitate people learning the skills to self-regulate, to be able to shift into that coherent state during life's challenges—you know, when the person cuts us off in traffic or the person in the staff meeting says that thing we know they are going to say that gets us upset—to be able, in that moment, to shift and self-regulate so that we can get into that more coherent state which then facilitates mental function. We can then make a more intelligent choice on how we deal with whatever the situation is at hand.

Now I know that was a long answer but I hope it gives you an idea of what we are talking about.

Dr. Dave: It's a great answer. Now, you mentioned the sympathetic and parasympathetic, and I am aware that there is a lot of new research interest in what is sometimes called the "third system"—I'm referring to the vagus system. I've interviewed Dr. Stephen Porges and also Dacher Keltner about the polyvagal theory, so it sounds like what you are referring to might relate to that. Does HeartMath somehow fit into that picture?

Dr. McCraty: It does. In fact I know Steve Porges, and he's more focused on the efferent or what is called the descending vagal system and how this reflects emotion and affects our ability to self-regulate. So it's very much aligned with what I am talking about. We are a little more focused on the afferent or the ascending information from the heart back to the brain. So it's related but different. But we facilitate or support each other's research, I would say.

Dr. Dave: OK. What is HeartMath's relationship to other approaches? For example, I'm thinking of the explosion of interest in positive psychology. There may be other approaches too that HeartMath overlaps with.

Dr. McCraty: Well, certainly, positive psychology would be related to our work. We were there a lot of years before the positive psychology movement ever occurred. In fact I spoke at the first positive psychology conference at the APA. Back when we started in the 1990s, there were maybe three or four papers in the research literature that had to do with positive emotions; there were very few. You are absolutely right that has exploded in recent years.

So it's related, but I think we are probably a little ahead of that curve in a way. Some of the questions that are asked in positive psychology…we have kind of already been there, done that and are on to giving people practical tools and techniques to actually self- regulate and become more positive.

Dr. Dave: Yeah, actually that's true of a number of people. I attended their most recent conference, and there are people who've been working more or less in the area of happiness and what broadly might be called positive psychology who've had research going on for 20 or 30 years.

Dr, McCraty: Yeah, and still asking questions like does it improve health? Do positive emotions still improve health? That's kind of like a no-brainer to me. There is so much research that shows that it does. So I think we are more focused on practical things that people actually can do, simple techniques that anyone can actually learn. For example, we've got programs that range from those for pre-school children with very positive outcomes all the way to training that we are doing for the military. The navy hired us for the Military Resilience Program. Really, who can't benefit from learning how to better self-regulate?

Dr. Dave: Do you have any data yet from that navy program?

Dr. McCraty: The work we have been doing over the last four years with the navy has been with deploying troops. We have trained probably about 5,000 people for a mission called the Cheney Operations, the most stressful job in the military. It has the highest risk of psychological injury of any job in the military. That's what the navy discovered. That's why they came to us. It's almost impossible or very, very difficult to do what I mean by research in a deployed population. But we have been able to get some indicators, leadership feedback being the primary one.

One of the more objective markers from that work has been the reduced number of sailors and soldiers on that mission on sleep medications. It was pretty routine that about 80 percent-plus of these men and women had to be on some kind of sleep meds. That program went through a number of improvements over the years as we learned more and more about how to do it in those populations. For the last couple of units being deployed, there have been almost no people on sleep meds. The effect that the program has had on many of the markers leadership cares about has been overwhelmingly positive. That's why the program has been supported and continued on.

Now we are doing an actual study here stateside in San Diego with a non-deploying population. And that study is not over yet, it's still ongoing. We did a control study and control groups and all the measures but we don't have the results yet. That's one of several studies ongoing now.

Dr. Dave: Yeah, that sounds fascinating! Are there any other current research programs that you can talk about, or ones that are planned for the future that you are hoping to do?

Dr. McCraty: Well, there's another one that's going on right now in fact. We are in the data analysis phase. It's a study where we monitored a group of about 25 people, monitored their heart rate variability for 24 hours a day for four or five months. Nothing has ever been done like this before, as far as I know—that kind of continuous recording. That's partly because of these new technologies that we have now, making it very easy to measure heart rate variability over long time periods. We'll analyze that data from a lot of different perspectives but the current study is to look at the interconnectedness between humanity and the earth's geomagnetic fields. Now that may sound a little wide, but there is an overwhelming amount of data about this. In fact one of our board members and collaborators named Franz Halberg—now you may know that name, but most people wouldn't…most people know the term *circadian rhythm*.

Dr. Dave: Yes.

Dr. McCraty: Dr. Halberg was the man who coined the term "circadian rhythm", and he's 93, still working seven days a week, sharp as a tack. He's a very passionate individual. In fact we published a few papers together here recently. He discovered, once he got onto the circadian rhythm and all the different aspects of it—and there is no greater world expert than Dr. Halberg on this—that our internal rhythms are affected by external things. That kind of ties in with the energetic sensitivity I was talking about earlier.

With the earth's magnetic field, our blood pressure, our heart rate and some of our hormonal levels are actually synchronized to it. When the external field gets disturbed, this usually hits people more in their emotional system. So when the planetary field environment is disturbed, people tend to get more mentally confused, get frustrated and irritated quicker, have weird dreams, things like that.

In fact we did a study of 1,600 people a couple of years ago about this. And now we are doing research at the physiological level to try and understand what the mechanisms are for this at both the planetary and physiological level. This is primarily in the context of people learning that when we have these…I call them energetic influxes or disturbances…we don't have to be affected by them. We really can self-regulate, but helping people understand this is an important part of the process of what's going on. That's a current study.

We've got another study started. One of the things that multiple studies have shown is that coherence training or HeartMath training is really helpful for blood pressure regulation. So for a lot of people with hypertension, even uncontrolled hypertension, HeartMaths is—I hate to use the word—almost magical in some cases in how well it works.

There are multiple studies on this. We are getting ready to do a much larger clinical study on hypertension and HRV (heart-rate variability) and coherence training.

Dr. Dave: You know, as you talk about Earth events affecting the heart, and through much of your discussion, I've been thinking about Dean Radin at the Institute of Noetic Sciences.

Dr. McCraty: Sure.

Dr. Dave: And I think there would be some mutual crossover in the research that you two are doing.

Dr. McCraty: Now, Dean's a friend. Are you talking about the global consciousness project work and the random number generators?

Dr. Dave: Yes.

Dr. McCraty: Yeah, sure. That's Roger Nelson who's the head of that, Dr. Nelson. Dean's closely involved, of course. In fact our lab is one of the nodes and sites for that system and has been almost since it began. I'm very aware of it. In fact both Dean and Roger are on the board for what we call the Global Law Coherence Initiative looking at the interconnection between humanity and the earth's systems. Part of what we are doing on that side of things is installing earth monitoring sites to look at the resonances in the earth's field, which is very different to the classical monitoring systems that are out there.

When you go to NOAA and different websites for magnetic fields, nobody has had a system which looks at the resonant frequencies in the earth's systems. It's bizarre to me that we don't have a federally funded system for it, because these are the resonances which overlap exactly with human brainwaves and heart frequencies and which are much more likely to explain the biological effects of these earth disturbances and earth fields that are well documented now. I'm kind of getting off track here, but anyway, we have the random number devices at each one of our monitoring sites as well. We are very closely aligned with Dean and Dr. Nelson on that project.

Dr. Dave: OK, since HeartMath does sell products and services, what products and or services does HeartMath offer? You've mentioned a couple but if you can just go over them again.

Dr. McCraty: Sure. Well it's probably important to know that there are two HeartMath organizations that work in alignment. There's the non-profit, which is the Institute of HeartMath who I am with. We do the research and work in education and also in communities. We have a number of training programs especially for community building. So these would be programs for law enforcement, fire departments, social services departments and so on. Also, we have a lot of programs for education and programs for kids of almost any age from school age almost all the way to college. That's on the non- profit side.

And then there's HeartMath LLC. They sell the devices I was talking about called em- Waves which do an objective measure of coherence. HeartMath LLC does clinical training programs for healthcare professionals and programs for hospital staff, and other types of training programs. They also sell a wide range of books, which are an easy way to get involved with HeartMath and an easy way to get started practicing the actual tools and techniques I've been referring to. So it's kind of a broad range. There is a deep set of products and technologies to help people learn how to be more in charge of themselves.

Dr. Dave: I'm wondering who your competitors are—part of it is for profit and usually people who are doing anything for profit do have competitors.

Dr. McCraty: You know that's a good question, and to be honest we really don't look at other people doing similar things as competitors. Our mission is to facilitate people in becoming more connected with their heart intuitions as we go through these changing times. There are other companies that have come out with similar technology to the em- Waves but to be honest we really look at them as helping us with our bigger mission.

Most of those companies have licensed our technology to do it anyway to make their products work.

For example, you'll never see us do comparative studies although others do so. We don't look at HeartMath versus psychotherapy or EMDR, those kinds of things, because we really believe that as we become more coherent it facilitates whatever you are doing. It's not really a competitive kind of worldview that we have. If we were going to do a study like that it would be more along the lines of, what are the benefits of combining HeartMath with X? It's probably not the answer you are looking for, but it's really kind of our worldview.

Dr. Dave: One category that just came to mind is sort of what you might call brain-wave drivers. They would also be looking at frequencies and a kind of co-herence related to the brain. Do you see some crossover or relationship there?

Dr. McCraty: In the neurofeedback community, which may be what you are referring to, that's an area where a lot of professionals who do neurofeedback have found that getting people heart coherent first really facilitates their train-ing sessions. So a lot of people doing EEG neurobiofeedback do HRV coherence training as part of that. You're right. Looking at brain activity, "coherence" is a term that's used there as well. We use it in the same way—I'm getting a bit too complex here—it's where you have got more than one EEG or brainwave site becoming synchronized. It turns out that when you become heart coherent, a natural result is increased brain synchronization, which is one of the things we published quite a few years ago. So a really a fast way to get the brain more in sync is to get the heart in sync. I don't know if I answered your question or not.

Dr. Dave: Oh yeah, definitely. What do you see is the future of HeartMath?

Dr. McCraty: Well, I think just continuing to expand like we are and developing the applications of it. On the technology side we're working now towards what we call group coherence, so that groups of people can, through technology, be working together. This is in addition to their personal level of coherence. What's the coherence at the group level? Those will be some of the future studies we are already looking at doing.

We already have a lot of data from organizations that when a team becomes more coherent together, there are a lot of organizational benefits that come out of it. For example, in many, many hospitals HeartMath is now the official training for the staff. The Mayo Clinic and many, many hospitals are doing this. Their absenteeism and turnover rates drop dramatically and performance improves in many different areas. There are reduced medical errors and meetings take about half the time. A lot of companies will say that when they really get coherent as a team, the amount of time they have to spend in meetings becomes dramatically reduced, for example.

Dr. Dave: Wow!

Dr. McCraty: Things like that, those kinds of studies—actually measuring coherence at the group level and associating this with the kinds of outcomes people are seeing.

Dr. Dave: Having been chair of a psychology department, I could see that having a tool like that would have been really useful.

Dr. McCraty: I understand, yes. I think everybody feels like they have too many meetings.

Dr. Dave: Now, I recall you also appeared in the wonderful film *I Am*. I got to see a showing in Marin County which Tom Shadyac, the director, presented. What can you tell us about your experience of being in that film?

Dr. McCraty: Oh, that was a kick. I am actually in about seven or eight films like that now. *I Am* is one of the more popular ones that made it into the theatres. Tom was a kick, I really enjoyed working with him.

Dr. Dave: Yeah, a really dynamic personality as we experienced him. As we wind down here, I wonder if there are any final points you'd like to make?

Dr. McCraty: Well I mean, I could talk for days, literally, here. I think we have covered it pretty well. My main message is that as people learn to become more heart centered, there are ways to access a deeper intelligence which helps us be more of who we really are—which I think is what people are really looking for, whether they would say it that way or not.

Dr. Dave: Well, great. Dr. Rollin McCraty, thanks for being my guest today on Shrink Rap Radio.

Dr. McCraty: One other thing—I remember the person who put us in connection said there was some kind of free document that your listeners could get. I'm not really familiar with it but I was just asked to mention it.

Dr. Dave: Yeah, I'm glad you've brought that up. There's a free e-book, and I will put a link to that in the show notes. Once again, I want to thank you.

Dr. McCraty: Do you have any questions? Or do you feel complete?

Dr. Dave: Well, one question that is still lingering for me is, I'm aware that there are some meditation approaches that focus on compassion and on the heart, and I don't know if you'd have something to say about that or not?

Dr. McCraty: Well, there have been a couple of studies. We were involved in one of them. We did the analysis and a couple of other ones that have found... you are referring more to some of the Buddhist practices, loving kindness and compassion?

Dr. Dave: Yes, exactly.

Dr. McCraty: One study that we've done looking at Buddhist monks found that monks who had been a monk for more than, I think it was three years, were walking around in the same state of coherence I was describing. This was measureable and the younger ones weren't in that state yet.

We also did a study here of a Buddhist community that is not too far away from us. And we got involved with UCLA and, in fact, we're doing the analysis for them. We found something very similar. As they were practicing meditations of loving kindness and compassion they also went into a coherent state. So it's really great. It's kind of another way of confirming what we are saying in a different population. And in a way it's similar. What we are really teaching is techniques for how you can shift into that coherent state in the moment that you are having a challenging situation.

Like I said, the person cuts us off in traffic or we have a traffic jam—it's a big issue for a lot of people. There's the traffic jam, and what the majority of people are doing, even if it's at a subtle level, is feeling impatient and upset, and all that's really doing is draining their vitality, their resilience, their energy. And it's not going to make the traffic move any faster. So it's really a way of taking charge of ourselves and saying, "Wait a minute, this doesn't make any sense! Here's a technique I can use to get myself, my system, into a state that adds energy instead of depletes energy, and connects me with more of my inner intelligence." That's an analogy for many things in life.

Dr. Dave: Dr. Rollin McCraty, thanks for being my guest today on Shrink Rap Radio.

Dr. McCraty: My pleasure.

(transcribed from www.ShrinkRapRadio.com by Elizabeth Hayes and copy edited by Geoff Hall)

SPOTLIGHT
DR. MYRON ROSS THURBER, PhD

Myron Thurber

I graduated with my first professional degree in physical therapy in 1987, after which I went to work in Yakima, Washington, at St. Elizabeth's hospital, where I was assigned to work out of the emergency room with patients with burns and wounds. I quickly learned to go emotionally numb to the unbearable pain of those I was working with in order to focus on cleaning and scrubbing their wounds. What I didn't realize at the time was that this process of learning to be emotionally numb would be a great detriment to my own relationships and health. In fact I didn't discover how to overcome this numbness until after I had finished my PhD and began to learn in greater depth about heart rate variability training through the Institute of HeartMath. This knowledge became a catalyst for me first to learn and then to teach how to better work with patients in mental, emotional, spiritual, and physical pain.

I continued to learn about treating patients with neurological disorders such as strokes and head injuries as well as sports and work-related injuries. One of the greatest lessons I ever learned was from an old military nurse and her protégé. On that day I was sitting at the nurses' station, doing paperwork, when these two women stopped and looked at each other. The older of the two said, "We better get ready". The other stopped, thought for a moment, and said, "You are right", and then they began putting together a burn treatment cart. Astoundingly, it was only a few minutes later that the computer printer produced an emergency order stating there had been a severe car accident, and that multiple occupants of the car had been severely burned. We were to prepare to receive the patients for treatment once the emergency vehicles arrived. I was stunned that these women had a way of knowing things that went beyond any academic training I had received. The older nurse explained that when she was in the military hospital unit she had herself learned and taught other nurses how to rely on the ability to know what was coming before a patient reached the hospital.

Since I had learned to speak Spanish as a missionary in Argentina, I had a lot of opportunities to work with migrant farm workers and consequently specialized in work-related injuries. I took advanced training in assessment to determine if, or when, and in what capacity, a worker could return to work. This specialization led me to Spokane, Washington and later to be an owner in Spokane

Industrial Rehabilitation. There I found time to listen to the stories and lives of the injured workers we were rehabilitating.

One day a client came into the clinic distraught and frustrated with the bureaucracy of returning to work when he felt he wasn't ready. He announced that he had a loaded gun in his truck, and that either he was going to kill the government worker he was frustrated with or commit suicide. I realized I didn't know how to handle the situation, and although I was able to calm him and help him resolve the situation, I was shaken. I also knew that I was struggling, having had a previous client commit suicide and another die to homicide. I decided then to take a few classes to learn how to work with suicidal and homicidal clients. After completing these, the professor asked if I would like to finish a Master's degree in psychology at Eastern Washington University, with an emphasis on mental health counseling. I did my internship at Shriner's Hospital, working with traumatized children using art, play, and relaxation techniques. In my physical therapy practice I continued to get increasingly complex cases to work with and continued to be more emotionally fatigued. I ended up agreeing to sell my business and took a break from physical therapy and mental health counseling for a year because I was burned out. A year later, in 2001, I went to work at St. Luke's Rehabilitation Institute, both as a physical therapist as well as a behavioral therapist, working primarily in the pain clinic. The person I replaced had provided biofeedback services for the patients, and I was expected to work towards becoming certified in general biofeedback. I had had some prior exposure to biofeedback, but not to the extent they needed. I began further training on biofeedback through the biofeedback International Alliance and was certified that same year (2001). During that training I was introduced to heart rate variability training and immediately saw how the application could be applied to the population I was working with. I was also introduced to EEG-based neurotherapy. Thus I used the biofeedback equipment and HeartMath tools to work with stressed hospital staff as well as the patients; I used them in my counseling office, the therapy gym, at the patient's bedside, and in the cardiac rehabilitation unit. What I longed for was a mentor—a mentor to help me understand why some patients didn't progress like I wanted and when to continue and when to stop treatment.

One day I had a feeling that I needed to go back to school again. When I asked my wife what she thought, she said, "I always thought you would". My children agreed and so I moved my family to Denton, Texas where I attended the University of North Texas and finished my PhD in counseling with an emphasis on rehabilitation. They had a biofeedback lab as well as a neurofeedback lab at the university, and both were equipped with heart rate variability equipment. For me, the most powerful learning experience wasn't any class but the Friday lunch meetings with the students, faculty and staff, who would gather and do grand rounds and case studies together. This was what I yearned for in a learning environment. Dr. Eugenia Bodenhamer-Davis was my mentor; she taught me to understand and listen to data as well as the instinctual and intuition feelings that I had seen in the nurses preparing for patients with burns; and to be quiet and to listen to the wisdom of my heart. My dissertation work was teaching HeartMath techniques using heart rate variability training for music performance anxiety. To prepare for the research study, I traveled to Boulder Creek, California and did training at the Institute of HeartMath and drank in their understanding of the heart, and the intelligence and power that could be harnessed. During my time there I experienced a change and learned that numb was not an emotion but rather a coping strategy I wanted to replace. I learned to feel again a wider and deeper range of emotion.

After graduating with my PhD and starting Neurotherapy Northwest in Spokane, Washington, I was contacted by the Institute of HeartMath and HeartMath LLC to help write the manual and later teach *The HeartMath Interventions Program* for health care providers. We have trained professionals from all over the world to use heart rate variability training to enhance their own professional practices and to apply it to a multitude of medical conditions. I have used it in prisons, hospitals, private practice, schools, camps, and sports and performance venues, but the place I love to apply it most is at home and to feel at peace in my body rather than numb.

I am co-owner of Neurotherapy Northwest, which provides biofeedback, neurofeedback, marriage, and family counseling, and we are expanding to include therapeutic tutoring, parenting classes, art therapy, and auditory and movement-based therapies as well. I am also developing along with Sketch for Schools a Neurodevelopmental Drawing Series to help integrate fine motor coordination in a systematic and developmental sequence. I am Chairman of the board for the non-profit organization "SAVY" Stop America's Violent Youth. We provide resources for treating children with Reactive Attachment Disorder, and their families, as well as training and education for professionals who work with this population.

LISTEN CLOSELY:
HEARING YOUR HEARTSONGS

Jennifer Lipski

We are social creatures. We seek interaction, and we communicate, working to understand each other in a myriad of ways. We observe body language, we get a sense of a person's energy, and we LISTEN to what is being said. *Or do we?*

Listening is vastly more than just audition, and it is the antithesis of statically attaining the same minds of others. Deeply attending to what is being communicated holds enormous dynamic potential for both the speaker and the listener; via the voice, a thought becomes an action, allowing the possibility of a reaction via a response. The listener is given the cherished role of learning, knowing, and experiencing the speaker, and the speaker can more fully allow each idea layer to unfold and blossom as it touches the air. What has the ability to occur is an exploration of the space that exists around us, as well as within us.

Communicating is a dichotomy of discovery; there is a giver and a receiver, and the roles are ever shifting. Babies coo and gurgle, and their parents lean in, watching and hearing, feeling into those sounds and the spaces between them. And so it begins: in our very nature, we seek to be understood, and we seek to understand.

While interacting is inherent in our human nature, seeking and attaining a deep understanding of one another is a continual duet that requires consistent attention and focus. There undoubtedly have been times when each of us has just stopped listening. Life can get hectic and messy, and it may be difficult to set aside strong emotions and distractions, as our rambling, discursive minds dissuade us from paying attention. We may revert to roles that no longer serve in healthy, productive ways, or we may seek to power a different view.

When active listening ceases, it is then that insufficiencies and insecurities begin. The spaces between us widen and fracture, effective communication grinds to a halt, and misunderstandings flourish. Listening is vital for learning, and achieving an understanding is the most precious bridge that crosses and closes the chasm.

To be able to hear, we must fully let go of agenda; when we seek to set an influence, we become rigid, casting limitations. But by observing, and then adjusting to balance that delicately swaying inner personal pendulum, the more easily we can tune in and understand. When we touch our own central place of knowing, our inherently fluid energy allows us to adjust amid the entropy. By extrapolation, listening makes space for the fullest perspective to occur, and allows the possibility of exponential expansion as it values and respects the most full and complete essence of the other. We must generously trust and welcome that which is being shared, recognizing it not only with our minds, but also with our hearts. Quintessentially, then, listening is deeply connecting with another.

Before a fruitful exchange can occur, however, the first caveat is self-knowing, which includes recognizing and honoring our own feelings, which are a "conscious awareness of emotions" (Freedberg & Gallese, 2007). Without this introspective and unabashed understanding of our selves, it is impossible to really listen and comprehend others, because "unless you can admit your own emotions, listening will be impossible" (Donohue & Seigel, 2005). And, just as above, so below: all of the concepts regarding outer dialogue is equally applicable when tuning in to listen to our own hearts and to the songs that are sung there by our unique inner voices. No one else can ever know exactly what our hearts say, how they say it, or what they make us feel – it is a uniquely personal experience. In this way, our hearts are our own private sirens and saints, omnipresent and available to guide us through every moment.

Our hearts are the speaker, and we are the listener. It is in this way that the same barriers that impede hearing others can also interfere with us hearing ourselves. Life can be frenetic and loud, our inner and outer states ungrounded, or we may repeat patterns that no longer serve us. If we want to lead heart-centered lives, we must check in with ourselves, and address that which acts as an impedance. But we do not just do this once, and then assimilate everything from that renewed yet singularly stationary point. As we change with each moment and every experience, communicating with ourselves is a lifelong journey that we must permit, lean into and explore. We will naturally ebb and flow, but it is not about seeking to be something or wanting to become someone; it is actually our inner sacred and energetic beings that already fully exist that we must allow to continually emerge, expanding. If we seek to nurture our internal language, we become increasingly self-aware, and move, guided by our hearts; we become agents of transformation and evolution. And then, when we focus beyond ourselves, we experience the eloquence of empathy. We are all a part of someone else; thus we learn and grow through moments of shared meaning, because "we are in the world, and the world is in us" (Whitehead, 1938). Structurally, our hearts communicate with our brains "influencing emotional processing as well as higher cognitive faculties such as attention, perception, memory, and problem-solving. In other words, not only does the heart respond to the brain, but the brain continuously responds to the heart" (Harrold, 2013). These hollow, muscular structures secured within our ribcages are vital metronomes, beating in time, calling our minds and bodies to respond. This enormous epicenter maneuvers us through this world, acting as compass and connector. It is also our teacher: "…the heart seems to have the ability to store memories… there is good evidence that the heart has an important role in how we learn from experience" (Reed & English, 2000). Listening deeply to our hearts is an unequivocal source of knowing; it allows us to part the veils and see beyond all measure: "…the heart can also be as a crossroad of consciousness, where energy from the belly center unites with the concentrated focus of the mind" (Palmer, 1998). Our sentient hearts radiate inner knowing throughout our bodies, and it is our obligation, then, to listen and respond: "attention is born from within – within the great esoteric traditions, attention is of divine origin" (Van Laer).

The heart has its' reasons
which reason cannot know.

-Pascal

There are countless colloquial phrases used in conjunction with communication from the heart. Dr. Henry Reed has stated that many of his research participants mention a "heart connection", and indeed: "…our language has many examples of the use of the word heart as a metaphor for intuition, as in 'I know in my heart' and for intuitive connections, such as 'my heart reached out to him'" (Reed, 2008). Our hearts are also a metaphor for living: we can only physically live while they pump essential life-blood through our bodies, and we can only fully thrive by uniting with their energetic streams, as well. "There is a long tradition that attributes to the heart…a synonym for the intuitive imagination…to perceive "subtle energy" or similar phenomena that are not visible to the senses" (Reed, 2008). There are the familiar phrases we may often hear and likely even have said: "to know something by heart" and "to follow your heart." These are not random strings of words. This knowledge is a part of who we are, and includes the intuitive spark of knowing from within.

For clarity and guidance in that which we fill our days, all we have to do is check in with ourselves, and take a quiet deep dive inside, because "our bodies speak volumes…knowing is binary…when you are clear, it is either a yes or a no" (Pierce, 1997). With a positive response [a 'yes'] from the body, people can experience different sensations, such as a warmth that spreads across the chest, a tingling in the abdomen to chest, or even a welling from the chest to the throat. It is all about knowing your "truth signals" (Pierce, 1997).

The quieter you become,
the more you hear.

-Rumi

We can all tap into our inner knowing. By practicing gentle and open self-awareness, this information is available to us at all times if we just listen. So right now, soften the focus of your eyes, drop and relax your shoulders. Bring your attention to anything physical you may feel, and release it, allowing your body to settle. Bring directed attention to whatever is on your mind, one thing at a time, and let each piece go, allowing yourself to just *be*. Know that there is *nothing else* at this precise moment that needs your complete attention other than your heart. Now quiet your breath; breathe softly and gently.

And LISTEN. Drop inside yourself, be still, and actually *listen to your own heart beating*. Hear its' strength and resonance. That is YOUR heart beating. It is only yours and no one else's. It has the power to bring your whatever strength you need.

While you are on the inside, imagine that you can touch the spaces around your heart. What does it feel like? Is it tender, hard, sensitive? Do you want to keep pressing there, or do you want to pull away? Pay attention to what your body is telling you. Only you can interpret these signals.

And again, while you are on the inside, what are the messages that you hear? What are your heart and body telling you? Is what you are receiving clear or jumbled? What can you do to be able to hear yourself more easily?

Lastly, in learning to explore these messages, our heartsongs, we must be sensitive to the needs of our hearts to expand and contract with us and our days: "…in a naïve way we might imagine our hearts can stay open like a giant sunflower…but our hearts have their rhythms and cycles…sometimes opening and closing like the blossoms of a flower…on a cool evening" (Kornfield, 1993). Allowing these fluctuations to occur is necessary to rejuvenate the heart and spirit, allowing our inner pendulum to readjust and our inner energy to renew.

It is only with the heart that one can see rightly;
what is essential is invisible to the eye.

-Antoine de Saint-Exupery, The Little Prince

Gentle suggestions to continue
HEARING YOUR HEARTSONGS:

1.) We must know and recognize that listening, and the knowledge that comes with it, is ALWAYS AVAILABLE to us. Whether within or without, all we have to do is be present, grateful and willing to receive.
2.) Where does the mountain end and the earth begin? WHERE DO YOU START, AND I END? That is key to remember - - in deeply listening, there is no end; it is a precious, continual connection of recognition and awareness.
3.) Know that YOU ARE ENOUGH. You are deserving of the brilliant heart that beats within you. Show up with your fullest expression, each day, every day.
4.) The GIFT OF BREATH allows us to shift and refocus. If you find yourself to be in a place of disconnect, remind yourself to breathe, and then reconnect with your heart. Trust the flow of your breath to guide you there.
5.) LISTEN CLOSELY, as often as you can. Listen closely to the song your heart sings, for it sings it only to you.

References:

Donoghue, P., & Siegel, M. (2005). *Are you really listening?: Keys to successful communication.* Notre Dame, IN: Sorin Books.

Freedberg, D., & Galesse, V. (2007). Motion, emotion and empathy in the esthetic experience. *Trends in cognitive science. 11* (5): p 197-203.

Harrold, Ed. (2013). The heart and brain connection and the role of emotions. Retrieved from: http://centerforwholeselfhealth.com/the-heart-brain-connection-the-role-of-emotions/

Palmer, H. (Ed.). (1998). *Inner knowing.* New York, NY: Tarcher/Putnam.

Kornfield, J. (1993). *A path with heart.* New York, NY: Bantam Books.

Pierce, P. (1997). *The intuitive way: A guide to living from inner wisdom.* Oregon, WA: Beyond Words Publishing, Inc.

Reed, H. (2008). *When hearts are joined: My story of our interconnectedness through intuition.* ReVision, Volume 31, No. 1 Retrieved from: http://moodle.atlanticuniv.edu/mod/resource/view.php?id=10363

Reed, H. , & English, B. (2000). *The intuitive heart: How to trust your intuition for guidance and healing* (Kindle DX version). Retrieved from Amazon: http://

www.amazon.com/dp/B00EA6TY70/ref=rdr_kindle_ext_tmb

Van Laer, L. (n.d.). Inner wisdom. *Parabola Magazine.* Retrieved from: http://www.parabola.org/index.php?option=com_content&view=article&id=360:the-beginning-of-wisdom

Whitehead, A.N. (1938). Nature alive. Lecture Eight in *Modes of Thought.* New York, NY: Macmillan. Retrieved from: https://www.brocku.ca/MeadProject/Whitehead/Whitehead_1938/1938_08.html

Jennifer Lipski is an RN, with a BS in Technical & Science Communications, and is currently completing an MA in Transpersonal Psychology. She is a creative writer, editor, researcher, avid home cook, animal advocate, and currently hosts the video conversation series "8 Minutes of Awesome. " Her personal message: "It's a heart-shaped world." She welcomes your comments! Contact her via http://www.8minutesofAwesome.com or http://www.facebook.com/JenniferMMW

Heart Health and Brain Health

Archibald Bower

Who would think that the heart has an effect upon your cognitive functioning? Of course, the ancient Greeks and Egyptians placed much importance on the heart as the main seat of the soul and a debate went on between cardiocentrists and cerebrocentrists. For the Egyptians the brain was removed through the nose but the heart (more important) was handled carefully. In recent years many studies have associated poor cardiovascular (CV) functioning with a host of mental disorders (depression, stress, schizophrenia, etc). All have a correlation with poor CV functioning. The mediators could be various ,e. g., poor diet, lack of exercise, drug effects, and genetic factors.

But today I am asking you to take the view that a sound body (i. e., a strong healthy heart) leads to a sound mind (i. e., efficient brain functioning).

In June 2014 a study out of Wake Forest Baptist Medical Center, in Winston-Salem, North Carolina, USA suggests that cardiovascular disease (CVD) is playing a role in declining cognitive functioning before it is clinically obvious. While there has been considerable research examining links between type 2 diabetes and increased risk for dementia, this research is the first to look at subclinical CVD and its role in cognitive dysfunction. According to the lead researcher, Dr. Hugenschmidt, "Our research shows that CVD risk caused by diabetes even before it's at a clinically treatable level might be bad for your brain."

"The results imply that additional CVD factors, especially calcified plaque and vascular status, and not diabetes status alone, are major contributors to type 2 diabetes related cognitive decline."

The findings are associated with the Diabetes Heart Study-Mind (DHS-Mind) in North Carolina which had been ongoing from 1998 to 2006. The researchers followed as many of the original 1,443 DHS study participants as possible who had cardiovascular measures. Of the available 516 subjects, 422 were affected with type 2 diabetes and 94 were not affected. This group was administered a battery of cognitive tests to evaluate a variety of different cognitive functions. Measures were taken of processes like attention, memory and processing speed. Others looked at executive functions which tap processes like managing time and attention, planning and organizing. These mental skills are typically associated with the frontal cortex of the brain. The results supported the conclusion that cardiovascular disease CVD is playing a role in declining cognitive functioning before it is clinically obvious.

Another report in June 2014 further adds support to the connection between a healthy heart and a well functioning brain. According to Health Day News (June 11) a report was published online in the Journal of the American Heart Association, supporting this contention. The study involved about 17,800 Americans from 45 years and up. They received a series of mental tests at the start of the research and again four years later. Statistical adjustments were made for differences in sex, age, education and race. The researchers found increasing deficits in learning, memory and verbal skills for nearly 10% of the participants. Severity of the deficits was related with heart functioning. Deficits in memory and learning were observed in 4.6 % of participants with the poorest heart health, 2.7 % of those with intermediate heart health and 2.6 % of the participants with the most healthy hearts.

According to the lead investigator, Dr. Evan Thacker of Brigham Young University, of Utah, "Even when ideal cardiovascular health is not achieved, intermediate levels of cardiovascular health are preferable to low levels for better [mental] function,"

Dr Thacker went on to clarify his statement, "This is an encouraging message because intermediate cardiovascular health is a more realistic target for many individuals than ideal cardiovascular health."

You may wonder what groups fared best? The researchers reported that better heart health and cardiovascular health was more frequent among men, people with higher education and higher incomes.

Conversely, the researchers found that mental impairments occurred more frequently among participants with lower incomes, those who already had a history of heart disease, and participants from the "stroke belt" states (mainly in southeastern USA).

However, just because there is a positive association between good heart health and good brain function does not mean that a healthy heart directly causes good brain function. One possibility according the Dr Thacker is that small strokes that did not result in observable symptoms played a role.

Next let us hear a few words from Ralph Sacco, M.D., chief of neurology at the Miller School of Medicine at the University of Miami and past president of the American Heart Association on the connection between heart health and brain health. He says, "New studies have shown that the risk factors for heart disease and stroke, such as physical inactivity and obesity, also contribute to dementia, Alzheimer's disease, memory loss and cognitive dysfunction."

Most of the public do not understand the connection between the two. However, over time unhealthy behaviours (poor diet, alcohol, and inactivity) take their toll on the cardiovascular system. They can result in the narrowing of blood vessels due to the accumulation of plaque and debris in the blood system. This reduces the blood flowing to the brain and is associated with hardening of the arteries in the heart and brain. Because the brain does not get the blood and oxygen it needs dysfunctions will occur in your cognitive abilities. As Dr Sacco says , " You could experience problems thinking, trouble with memory, difficulty finding your way from place to place…" And of course there is an increase in the danger of a stroke should the blood flow to the brain be abruptly blocked.

Many people associate memory loss with Alzheimer's disease and believe that it can not be treated or prevented. However, Dr Sacco, as president of the American Heart Association , observes that by caring for your heart by controlling the well known risk factors you can also have a profound effect upon the health of your brain.

A report on June 18, 2014 notes that Australia is in the midst of a heart failure epidemic. Researchers state that 5% of the population have heart failure. The study reports that 500,000 Australians have the condition, up from 350,000 in 2002.

The research leader Professor Simon Stewart of the Baker IDI Heart & Diabetes Institute says that heart failure is not the same as a heart attack. Rather it is a chronic event stretching over time during which the heart struggles to pump enough blood through the body. Symptoms are shortness of breath, fatigue and sleeping difficulties. While heart failure can be treated there is permanent damage to the heart and likely damage to the kidneys and brain.

As heart failure progresses the person will be hospitalized. At this point their general health often deteriorates rapidly. They have less chance of living five more years than a woman with breast cancer.

In conclusion, it appears clear that a healthy CV system is important for healthy brain functioning. Keeping the body healthy through life long habits of exercise and diet will have benefits for the majority of people as they pass into older age.

Sources :

http://www.wakehealth.edu/News-Releases/2013/Heart_Health_Matters_to_ Your_Brain.htm

Mental Disorders Across the Adult Life Course and Future Coronary Heart Disease: Evidence for General Susceptibility, Catherine R. Gale, et al., *Circulation*, published online November 2013

Dr Sacco, American Heart Association http://www.nlm.nih.gov/medlineplus/ news/fullstory_146755.html

Australia heart epidemic: http://news.ninemsn.com.au/ health/2014/06/19/00/09/australia-faces-heart-failure-epidemic

THE HEART: KING OF ORGANS

(un appel à une révolution médicale)

Abdullah A. Al Abdulgader

The explosive technical advances of the 20th century were not without significant drawbacks in our interpretation of scientific knowledge. A prominent example of this was the sense of the human heart as merely a pump. In contrast to the understanding of the heart previously recognized by the most important civilizations in human history, the cardiac sciences in the 20th century deprived the heart of its pivotal role as the seat of the emotions in learning, decision-making, and intuition, which had been the implicit understanding of ancient civilizations. The heart is a sensory organ, and it acts as a sophisticated information encoding and processing center that enables it to learn, remember and make independent functional decisions. In 2014, therefore, it is somewhat embarrassing to practice in the cardiac sciences without acknowledging the electromagnetic, neuro-cardiac, biophysical, and energetic interactions of the human heart with the surrounding environment. Our new perspective is to see the human heart as the center of a spectrum of sciences ranging from genes to galaxies.

The weight of scientific evidence supporting the view that the human heart has different mechanistic interactions with its surroundings is increasing—interactions as near to the heart as other body organs and as far away as the planetary orbits and solar flares. The human heart is a sensitive detector, which is reactive to geological, geophysical, and astrophysical changes. This fact is unavoidable if we are prepared to discover the mysteries of the human heart in health and disease.

In the language of mainstream cardiology today, cardiac memory refers to T-wave changes induced by ventricular pacing, or arrhythmia, which accumulates in magnitude and duration with repeated episodes of abnormal activity. Cardiac memory can also be interpreted in terms of ventricular action potential. Our current vision of neuro-cardiology and modern psychophysiological research requires new theories in order to encompass a wider understanding of cardiac memory as the principal memory involved in information processing and human behavior. This new perspective is a good reason to focus not only *retrospectively* but also *prospectively* on the mostly neglected scenarios of psychobehavioral changes in heart transplant recipients.

Chronobiologically interpreted, ambulatory blood pressure and heart rate monitoring is a new visionary practice with true potential to revolutionize risk aversion strategies in treating heart disease. It renders the diagnosis of hypertension more reliable and detects otherwise undiagnosed severe diseases such as exaggerated diurnal over swing that can occur with or without an elevation of mean blood pressure. The implementation of this new philosophy assumes that, in the near future, the administration of medications to treat heart disease should be optimized along the circadian scale. Even social diseases like war, terrorism, and crime, and natural cataclysms like earthquakes can be analyzed and forecast utilizing sensitive physiological parameters such as systolic blood pressure and heart rate variability.

The persistent false perception of the human heart as merely a pump in isolation from the surrounding environment creates major gaps in our knowledge towards better understanding the etiology and patho-mechanisms of cardiac disease. Cardiovascular disease is still at the top of the list as a major killer worldwide, yet it is hardly surprising that meta-analysis reviews looking at the outcomes of modern interventions in the treatment of heart disease in the last 30 years have not shown any significant improvements in long-term morbidity and mortality rates.

Our new understanding of the science of heart rate variability and its spectrum of frequencies that have significant correlations to solar activity is breaking news in the history of science, and this needs to be translated into clinical practice to minimize, or destroy, the burden of heart disease in nations and individuals. For example, the efficient application of heart rate modulation techniques, such as electro-stimulation and prescribing frequencies that utilize the power of modifying the heart's rhythm to treat heart disease, herald a new era in medical history to treat the body by the body and by the physics of nature. Our success in treating systemic hypertension in the short term by utilizing this concept of cardiac coherence should encourage the world's medical communities to adopt these new and safe therapeutic modalities. Furthermore, shifting people and individuals to a more frequent cardiac coherent state should increase our intuitive intelligence and collective consciousness and consequently activate our innate emotions to spread love, compassion, and mercy.

Even the pumping functions of the heart should be exposed to a scientific critique. The failure of the heart's pumping function in congestive heart failure is currently creating major health and economic problems in individuals as well as all nations, but research in a few medical centers around the world to develop more efficient ventricular assistive devices will not be able to provide an efficient alternative to the human heart without incorporating this new understanding of the heart as a major sensory organ. Indeed, it is impossible to provide the sole power for the 100,000 km of the human circulation journey merely according to the rules of mechanical physics for assessing myocardial wall stress.

The human circulatory system is unique in that, in an upright position, the heart is located 130-160 cm above the ground while the brain, which needs to be constantly perfused by blood, is 30-40 cm higher. Blood tends to accumulate in the organs that lie below the heart and needs to be transported back to the heart against the forces of gravity for normal diastolic functions. The extreme paucity of research in diastolic dysfunction—and its correlation to the philosophy of quantum gravity—is another major obstacle to a proper understanding of the pathophysiology of congestive heart failure, which needs to be immediately addressed. The changing physiology of the human heart in microgravity, and increased gravity in the environment, may contribute to our knowledge in this direction. The role of the heart's electromagnetic field, and the quantum physics driving the gravito-electromagnetic forces that enable the heart to control circulation with extraordinary ease and a delicate equilibrium, should be explored by scientists as a top priority.

The consequences of these new discoveries of the heart as the master of the psychophysiology of the human body and its external interactions are tremendous. One of the major consequences is its contribution to decisions on the termination of human life in the case of individuals who are claimed to be brain dead. Major discussions on this issue occurred at high-ranking religious and legislative levels in different countries following the recommendations of the King of Organs Conferences in Saudi Arabia in 2006, 2008, 2010 and 2012. The practice of considering the absence of cortical function as true death, in the presence of a functioning cardiovascular system, should be submitted to immediate revision in all countries, in view of the newly recognized role of the human heart. This new understanding should herald new hopes of mercy on the horizon, to alleviate an agony extending back to 1969.

The fact that the human heart is the largest and most dominant generator of the electromagnetic field in the body has potential major implications in regenerative medicine. Heart sound and magnetic field may work together to establish what we call an information, or morphogenetic field, which is driving the fate of our organs during organogenesis. Physical stimuli, including magnetic field and sound frequencies as nano-mechanical energy, affect cell behavior including stem cell commitment and terminal differentiation quite remarkably, without the intervention of chemical agonists or viral vector mediated gene delivery.

We assume that the human heart as the principal biological generator of the pulsating electromagnetic field with its associated frequencies should make a significant contribution to the superposed quantum states of different space–time geometry and quantum gravity, giving rise to individual as well as global consciousness. This understanding is stressed by the fact that conscious-ness-shift occurs immediately after the cessation of heart beats.

This new philosophy in the cardiac sciences should bring both cardiologist and physicist closer to the ancient wisdom—that the human heart is the master of the emotions, and behavior, and the seat of the soul. There is no true reason to prevent the existence of a new hybrid knowledge between modern science and ancient wisdom, which is expected to generate a visionary future in the practice of cardiology. Immam Algazaly (1058-1111 BC) in his famous book, *Wonders of the Heart*, highlights astonishing insights into the true role of the human heart. The modern and state-of-the-art cardiac sciences, which we are calling for, are just now at the threshold of what Imam Algazaly wrote, around one thousand years ago.

Miraculous and paranormal definitions, which were considered taboo in all religions and cultures in the past, and which included the spirit, the soul, and its true interactions with the human heart, should be closer to our understanding. The coherent narrative stream of the rule of the heart and its connections to the underlying universe, which we perceive through our consciousness, is a deeper call for higher wisdom. This is not a simple alert to change but a serious call for revolution.

Prof. Abdullah A. Al Abdulgader:

MBBS(KSA)-DCH(Ireland)-DCH(Edin)-MRCP(UK)-ABP-FRCP(Edin), Diploma of Honor(Board of the International Committee GEOCHANGE);
Senior Congenital Cardiologist-Robotic Electrophysiologist;
World Gold medal Awardee(WOS-CO-2012);
Founder and President of The International Conference in Advanced Cardiac Sciences (King of Organs);
Scientific Advisory Board Member(Heart Math Institute-USA);
Scientific Board Member(Global Coherence Initiative-USA);
General Director of Research Center(Eastern Province-Saudi Arabia).

INDEX

154

INTERNATIONAL JOURNAL OF
NEUROPSYCHOTHERAPY

IJNPT

The International Journal of Neuropsychotherapy (IJNPT) is an open-access, online journal that considers manuscripts on all aspects of integrative biopsychosocial issues related to psychotherapy. IJNPT aims to explore the neurological and other biological underpinnings of mental states and disorders to advance the therapeutic practice of psychotherapy.

Visit **www.neuropsychotherapist.com/submissionscall/**

for more information on submitting articles, letters and research notes.

www.neuropsychotherapist.com/journal/

The Neuropsychotherapist

We are your online source for news and information about the emerging field of Neuropsychotherapy and its community of professionals.

We aim to bring together researchers and practitioners in this multi-disciplinary field to share their latest findings and experiences.

Subscribe for exclusive access to the heart of our project: our monthly eMagazine. Feature articles from leading experts, news, reviews, and department columns on a wide range of subjects relevant to the progressive psychotherapist and integrative health care professional. While a member you have access to the complete archive of Members Only material including all of our magazine issues.

The Neuropsychotherapist eMagazine is presented as a digital online version and a downloadable PDF. These are interactive PDFs, so you can turn off the "image" layers to print just the text if you are reading the magazine in Adobe Reader. All feature articles are also presented as separate PDFs in A4 format for you to download and print.

Access to additional stand-alone articles(monographs) that are not visible to the general public. Also blog articles, news, reviews, opinion pieces, and more that are invisible to non-members. When you log in to the site, all of the hidden material will be available to you for as long as you have an active membership. For more details on membership benefits, see the comparison tables below.

When you consider all these features for as low as $8/quarter*, we believe it's amazing value for money!

NEUROPSYCHOTHERAPIST.COM

The MindScience Institute

Transforming information  into practice

mindscienceinstitute.com

The MindScience Institute has been set up to act as a networking hub for the wide array of activity occurring in the world. Based in Australia, it is hoped that pathways will be opened between my many friends and associates in the USA into the Asian region, the East and into Europe and back again. There are so many interesting and varied points of view and perspectives that are generated not only through styles of practice, but also cultural background. The MindScience Institute will look to provide education and information, but also share and link with the excellent programs and teaching already underway. The time is now ripe to translate and even transform the avalanche of information about the mind and brain and the interactions within the body and now the activity of our genes into the practice of health and healing. We can take practice into a new and, I'm sure, better place.

Richard Hill is the founder of the Mind Science Institute. He became fascinated by the science of the brain and mind after attending workshops by Daniel Siegel, Lou Cozolino and Ernest Rossi. He has been a student of human behaviour and the activities of the mind for many years before that. As a professional actor for the first 20 years of his career, a felt sense of being human and the art of truly 'getting into someone else's shoes' was the central focus of his life. The transition into counseling and psychotherapy seemed reasonable.

MindScience TV will brings conversations with experts from around the globe into the easy access of everyone with a computer. There are so many stories to tell and be told. The MindScience Institute is proud to help in spreading the news, sharing the information and becoming a networking hub.

Printed in Great Britain
by Amazon.co.uk, Ltd.,
Marston Gate.

10125386R00094